WITH THE
WHOLE
CHILD
IN MIND

WITH THE WHOLE CHILD IN MIND

Insights from the Comer School Development Program

Linda Darling-Hammond
Channa M. Cook-Harvey
Lisa Flook
Madelyn Gardner
Hanna Melnick

Alexandria, VA USA

1703 N. Beauregard St. • Alexandria, VA 22311-1714 USA
Phone: 800-933-2723 or 703-578-9600 • Fax: 703-575-5400
Website: www.ascd.org • E-mail: member@ascd.org
Author guidelines: www.ascd.org/write

Deborah S. Delisle, *Executive Director;* Stefani Roth, *Publisher;* Genny Ostertag, *Director, Content Acquisitions;* Susan Hills, *Acquisitions Editor;* Julie Houtz, *Director, Book Editing & Production;* Jamie Greene, *Associate Editor;* Judi Connelly, *Associate Art Director;* Donald Ely, *Senior Graphic Designer;* Mike Kalyan, *Director, Production Services;* Shajuan Martin, *E-Publishing Specialist;* Cynthia Stock, *Typesetter*

PAPERBACK ISBN: 978-1-4166-2694-7   ASCD product #119028   n10/18
PDF E-BOOK ISBN: 978-1-4166-2696-1; see Books in Print for other formats.
Quantity discounts: 10–49, 10%; 50+, 15%; 1,000+, special discounts (e-mail programteam@ascd.org or call 800-933-2723, ext. 5773, or 703-575-5773).
For desk copies, go to www.ascd.org/deskcopy.

Library of Congress Cataloging-in-Publication Data

Names: Darling-Hammond, Linda, 1951- author.
Title: With the whole child in mind : insights from the Comer school
    development program / Linda Darling-Hammond, Channa M. Cook-Harvey, Lisa
    Flook, Madelyn Gardner, Hanna Melnick.
Description: Alexandria, VA, USA : ASCD, [2019] | Includes bibliographical
    references and index.
Identifiers: LCCN 2018032905 (print) | LCCN 2018044120 (ebook) | ISBN
    9781416626961 (PDF) | ISBN 9781416626947 (pbk.)
Subjects: LCSH: School improvement programs—United States. | Educational
    change—United States. | Child development—United States. | Community and
    school—United States. | Comer, James P.
Classification: LCC LB2822.82 (ebook) | LCC LB2822.82 .D37 2018 (print) | DDC
    371.2/07—dc23
LC record available at https://lccn.loc.gov/2018032905

26 25 24 23 22 21 20 19   1 2 3 4 5 6 7 8 9 10 11 12

WITH THE WHOLE CHILD IN MIND

Foreword

Whenever I think of Dr. James Comer, two words quickly come to mind: *visionary* and *prophet*. As a newly minted child psychiatrist a half-century ago, he conceived and launched the School Development Program (SDP) in two low-performing elementary schools in New Haven, Connecticut. His audacious vision was to engage the key adults involved in the education and upbringing of children—from the principal and teachers to parents and caregivers—in a collaborative effort to foster the healthy development of students along six critical pathways, including cognitive, social, and psychological. Dr. Comer understood even then that these facets of youngsters' development were intertwined, interdependent, and mutually reinforcing. He also understood that if they progressed appropriately along these pathways, they were likelier to succeed in school and in life.

As Professor Linda Darling-Hammond, one of the nation's foremost experts on K–12 education, documents in this concise history of the origins, evolution, and impact of Dr. Comer's pioneering work, the SDP gradually gained traction during its first two decades. Then, in the late 1980s, the Rockefeller Foundation began providing substantial funding, which I orchestrated as its vice president. This support catapulted the SDP from 66 schools in 3 districts (in 1988) to more than 650 schools in 80 districts (by 1997). Rigorous evaluations have consistently shown impressive results when the SDP is faithfully implemented in schools and genuinely backed by the district.

Over the years, the SDP, which is the quintessential bottom-up approach to school improvement, has weathered the torrent of punitive top-down reforms imposed on public schools. These have ranged from tougher academic standards, high-stakes tests, and teacher accountability, to school choice, charter schools, and state and mayoral takeovers. As Professor Darling-Hammond reports, this incessant pressure from on high has generated skimpy academic gains for the students who languish furthest behind academically. The cascade of reforms has also left educators marginalized and jaded. Many parents are alienated and confused, while anxious and disenchanted students pine for more stimulating modes of schooling.

In 2015, Washington mercifully relaxed the pressure on local schools when it replaced the federal No Child Left Behind law with the Every Student Succeeds Act (ESSA). Although it has taken 50 years, teachers, principals, parents, students, policymakers, and employers have increasingly come to appreciate Dr. Comer's prescience. They all recognize the critical relationship of the development of youngsters' social and emotional skills to their success in school and subsequently in the labor force and in life.

Furthermore, as Professor Darling-Hammond writes, recent research into the science of learning affirms what Dr. Comer deeply understood at the very outset of SDP and what his approach has consistently demonstrated—namely, that cognitive and social-emotional development are tightly interrelated and that social and emotional development can bolster academic learning and performance. In 2016, the Aspen Institute founded the National Commission on Social, Emotional, and Academic Development (SEAD), whose objective is to generate local, state, and national momentum for the provision of high-quality social, emotional, and academic development in every school. Professor Darling-Hammond cochairs the commission, and Dr. Comer, quite fittingly, serves as its honorary chair. Thus, SEAD has finally come of age, steadfastly championed and painstakingly nurtured by its prophet, Dr. James Comer.

This book provides guidance to those who today are seeking to dramatically expand the whole child support system that Dr. Comer long ago understood and for which he developed a powerful schoolwide model. Hopefully, the new impetus for social-emotional and academic development will be informed and accelerated by his pioneering work so that many more schools can enable many more young people to reach their full potential in life.

Hugh B. Price
Former president and CEO of the National Urban League
Commissioner, National Commission on Social, Emotional, and
    Academic Development

1

Placing Child Development
at the Center

My dream was to go out into the real world and bring about school improvement at a level that would impact national thinking, practice, and policy. . . . We began with two of the lowest achieving, most troublesome elementary schools in the city. The usual focus at the time was on the students. But from my own experience, and my public health and child psychiatry background, I knew that we had to focus on the system and the child . . . not just the child.

–James P. Comer, Foreword to The Kids Got Smarter

When James Comer visited Baldwin Elementary School in New Haven, Connecticut, in the fall of 1968, his experience, as he described it, was shocking:

> On the first day of school, I walked down the hall at Baldwin School and I was almost attacked by a teacher in trouble. She was anxious, wild-eyed. She grabbed my arm and said, "Help me! Help me!" and literally pulled me into her classroom. What I saw was almost unbelievable. Children were yelling and screaming, milling around, hitting each other, calling each other names, and calling the teacher names. When the teacher called for order, she was ignored. When I called for order, I was ignored. That had never happened to me before. We headed for the hall, confused and in despair. Her classroom was not the only one in trouble.

The school was chaotic and noisy . . . teachers and administrators raced back and forth . . . teachers could not find supplies. . . . The first week was a short one—Thursday, September 5 and Friday, September 6. We left for the weekend shaken, with mixed feelings of impending doom and some vague hope that all would be better next week . . . my denial mechanisms were operating at top form. I suppose I just could not bear to admit the extent of the problem we had. (Comer, 1980, pp. 76–77)

Comer was then a young child psychiatrist at the Yale Child Study Center in New Haven, where he had just launched the School Development Program (SDP). Baldwin and King elementary schools, where Comer began his work, were among the lowest achieving of New Haven's 31 public schools. More than 50 percent of the students were on government assistance, students were chronically truant, student behavior was disruptive, and morale among the staff was low.

A few years later, however, the picture was very different. The schools had become peaceful, purposeful, and happy environments for children, welcoming to parents, and supportive of staff. A later analysis of achievement in the two New Haven pioneer schools found that between 1969 and 1984, 4th grade students' grade equivalent scores increased from about 3rd grade level in reading and math to 6th grade level in reading and 5th grade level in math. By 1984, these schools were two of the highest-performing schools in New Haven and had near-perfect attendance (Comer, 1988).

Although many rounds of school reform have come and gone in the 50 years since this work began, the School Development Program has withstood the test of time, quietly revolutionizing the purpose and organization of some of the most troubled schools in the United States, empowering teachers and parents as decision makers; fostering healthy development of students; and producing noteworthy outcomes for student behavior, positive attachment to school and adults, and achievement. The SDP builds on the science of child development, creating a whole child framework for reform that takes a systems approach toward reorganizing the school. It aims to ensure that all members of the school community—students, teachers, principals, parents, support providers—are knowledgeable about child development and supported in working together as interdependent, valued, and respected partners, simultaneously empowered to make decisions together for the express benefit of every child.

The School Development Program builds on and conveys shared professional knowledge about how children and adults develop and learn that should, in an ideal world, be readily available to every educator. It is not a cookie-cutter program, but rather a means for enabling educators and schools to support social, emotional, cognitive, and physical development for children—a foundational approach that research has found is critically important for success in both school and life (Cantor, Osher, Berg, Steyer, & Rose, 2018; Osher, Cantor, Berg, Steyer, & Rose, 2018).

This whole child approach has been difficult for many schools to engage in during the era of test-based accountability ushered in by the No Child Left Behind Act (NCLB), when U.S. education policies focused intently on raising student test scores, often to the exclusion of other goals, such as student health and welfare; physical, social, emotional, and psychological development; critical and creative thinking; and communication and collaboration abilities.

Under the threat of public shaming, staff firings, or school closures if scores did not climb each year, schools often adopted a "drill and kill," "test and punish," "no excuses" agenda that caused many of the nation's most vulnerable children to experience a narrowly defined, scripted curriculum and a hostile, compliance-oriented climate that pushed many of them out of school (Darling-Hammond, 2007). In this context, many schools were not focused on enabling students to acquire the broader life skills they need or the sense of self to achieve their full potential. For example, a 2006 study of more than 148,000 6th to 12th graders reported the following findings:

- Only 29 percent of the students felt their school provided a caring, encouraging environment.
- Fewer than half of the students reported they had social competencies such as empathy, decision-making skills, and conflict-resolution skills (from 29 percent to 45 percent, depending on the competency).
- Thirty percent of high school students reported engaging in multiple high-risk behaviors such as substance abuse, sex, violence, and attempted suicide. (Durlak, Weissberger, Dymnicki, Taylor, & Schellinger, 2011)

These conditions contribute to school failure and high dropout rates. Research shows that narrowly conceived, standardized, and punitive approaches to instruction and student treatment undermine student motivation and learning and facilitate student disengagement from school. Almost three-quarters of a million students in the United States—disproportionately students of color, those with disabilities, and those from low-income families—do not complete high school each year, costing society hundreds of thousands of dollars per student over the course of their lifetimes (Rumberger, 2012). The costs of this disengagement and the subsequent exclusion of students from educational opportunity are devastating and lasting for individuals and for society as a whole. Yet we know a great deal about how to support students and enable success by attending to their development in ways that foster relationships and promote learning.

At a time when the education world is seeking to recalibrate after the No Child Left Behind era, it is appropriate to refocus on how this kind of knowledge can be planted and nurtured in schools. This book offers an account of one well-vetted way to support the development of whole child education in the context of whole school reform. We connect this work to the emerging science of learning and development and the implications for practice of building schools in alignment with how children develop and learn.

The School Development Program

The School Development Program, also known as the Comer Model or Comer Process, was established in 1968 in two struggling elementary schools as a collaborative effort between the Yale Child Study Center and New Haven Public Schools. Since then, the SDP has been implemented in more than 1,000 schools in 26 states in the United States, the District of Columbia, Trinidad and Tobago, South Africa, England, and Ireland (see the Comer School Program website, https://medicine.yale.edu/childstudy/communitypartnerships/comer).

At the heart of the SDP approach is a value for relationships that are understood to provide the foundation for children's healthy development. This insight about the context for child development was what led Comer to his first epiphany about what a school improvement program might seek to do. His reflection started with a question:

> Why was I able, and why were my brothers and sisters and others who came from similar backgrounds able, to succeed in school and have opportunities when I had friends who were just as able but went downhill? They had different developmental experiences. Systems were created to pass on the [false] belief that our abilities are largely genetically determined. All the scientific evidence that has accumulated gets ignored because we keep focusing on curriculum, instruction, assessment. The education enterprise focuses on it, the public believes it, and practice confirms it—what you end up doing is showing that kids who are prepared for school receive support for development and do well, and those who are not, don't do well.

Comer emphasizes that if children are not doing well in school, or if they are behaving in ways that are counterproductive, adults must understand that the child is not trying to be "bad" but is exhibiting a need for attention—often related to deeper concerns that need to be surfaced and understood—or a need for explicit teaching about how to behave productively in the classroom context. When adults assume that children are deliberately misbehaving and jump to punishing the behavior rather than seeking to understand it and model alternatives, students fail to learn how to build a repertoire for problem solving. Furthermore, they can adopt an oppositional stance to the teacher and the school.

In schools that are underperforming, where students and adults are often trapped in a vicious cycle of frustration, isolation, and helplessness, Comer's process for school reform trains educators, in partnership with parents, to take specific, developmentally sound steps toward holistic school change that creates a productive context for each child's development. The goal is for all educators to use the principles of child and adolescent development to create positive interactions between students and school staff members, and ultimately to transform school culture by also drawing on family and community resources (Cook, Murphy, & Hunt, 2000).

The developmental pathways

The School Development Program focuses on six developmental pathways—cognitive, social, psychological, physical, linguistic, and ethical—as a foundation for successful learning and healthy development (see Figure 1.1). Educators and parents are provided with a framework that helps them support the healthy development of children along all six pathways by engaging in a coordinated set of student-support processes and by using three guiding principles for their own work: collaboration, consensus, and no-fault problem solving. With an approach to teaching, learning, and classroom and school management that is student-centered and developmentally appropriate, the program emphasizes the importance of reflection by both children and adults to promote better thinking, better management of feelings, and more desirable social behavior.

FIGURE 1.1 | The Developmental Pathways

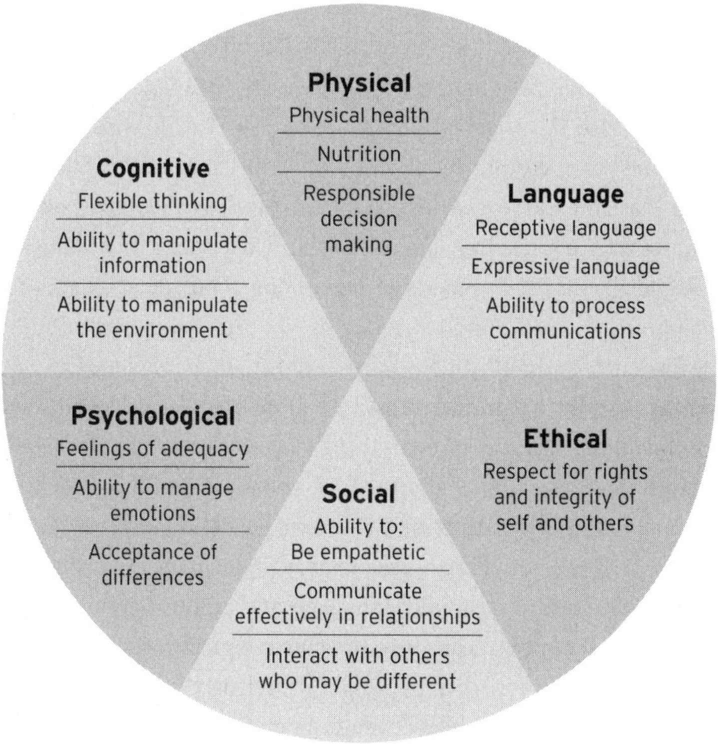

Physical
Physical health

Nutrition

Responsible decision making

Cognitive
Flexible thinking

Ability to manipulate information

Ability to manipulate the environment

Language
Receptive language

Expressive language

Ability to process communications

Psychological
Feelings of adequacy

Ability to manage emotions

Acceptance of differences

Social
Ability to:
Be empathetic

Communicate effectively in relationships

Interact with others who may be different

Ethical
Respect for rights and integrity of self and others

Source: From Yale Child Study Center, School Development Program. Copyright 2008 by Yale Child Study Center. Reprinted with permission.

In schools using the Comer Process, far more is expected from students than just cognitive development. Children's development is multifaceted, and children need support in developing their full repertoire of skills. As described in *Six Pathways to Healthy Child Development and Academic Success* (Comer, Joyner, & Ben-Avie, 2004), educators play a role in supporting children's development along multiple pathways.

Promoting the *physical* development of children and adolescents encompasses physical health, nutrition, and responsible decision making, especially regarding adolescent sexual conduct and use of drugs and alcohol. The *cognitive* pathway involves helping children and adolescents increase their capacity to think for themselves, to plan strategically and effectively, to solve problems in different contexts, to set goals for themselves, and to work with focused attention to accomplish those goals. This pathway also includes recognizing when one's own resources are not sufficient to carry out a task and when to ask for and receive help. A focus on the *psychological* pathway includes training children and adolescents to manage their emotions in socially acceptable ways and increasing their capacity for self-acceptance and self-confidence during the ongoing process of identity formation. Establishing a safe classroom climate is essential for students to grow in confidence and feel they can take risks and learn.

Language is a part of everything that occurs within the school. Communication skills—listening and speaking, reading and writing—are essential for students to become successful and productive in our diverse society. To ensure mastery of language, teachers must deliberately teach and model language and communication skills, for children do not all come into the classroom with the same exposure or experience with language. Promoting development along the *social* pathway involves developing children's and adolescents' capacity to build healthy relationships, to interact with individuals from diverse backgrounds, and to demonstrate empathy toward others. The *ethical* pathway is concerned with helping children and adolescents to develop the capacity for acting with justice and fairness toward themselves and others, including showing respect and having integrity. Encouraging students' involvement in designing the classroom codes for verbal and nonverbal behavior provides them with an opportunity to apply the ethical pathway to their everyday experience. Across all of these pathways, students benefit from having adult role models.

This framework helps educators and parents better understand their children and themselves, and it is used to address student, adult, and community issues. To promote children's academic success, the two most important objectives are developing a comprehensive understanding of what needs to be done in the best interests of every child, and then making the deliberate effort to meet the needs of every child effectively (Comer et al., 2004).

The developmental pathways framework can be used as part of the process of student planning, to understand developmental issues that children are experiencing using a whole child lens. For example, a child may sleep in class for reasons that are physical (lack of sleep), cognitive (boredom with the task), or psychological (to disguise feelings of inadequacy). The pathways approach encourages considering multiple causes and generating solutions without blame to address the needs of each child holistically. It can also be applied to curriculum, instruction, and classroom management. Teachers can categorize what they are doing according to the pathways to identify ways that they are supporting students' development along each pathway and brainstorm ways that they can augment support for any pathways as needed. Teachers can also use the pathways to assess their own well-being and interactions with students (Comer et al., 2004).

The pathways framework is also a guide for schools to assess programs that are being considered for implementation. For example, the School Planning and Management Team, which is part of the SDP structure, might examine a program by creating a grid that looks at the populations served and the pathways addressed to make sure the program is truly meeting the needs of students and addresses most, if not all, of the six pathways. Educating parents about the six pathways allows parents to understand their children more fully and to learn the benefits of interacting with them from a perspective of whole child development. The pathways framework provides teachers, students, and parents with a common language.

A child-focused developmental perspective extends the principle of no-fault problem solving to relationships with children;

provides a framework for adults to consider children's behavior in a larger context, offering a broader view of each child; and enables adults to develop and implement strategies to promote students' health and positive self-esteem. The goal is for educators to become facilitators of opportunities for success, so that students ultimately have good reason to see themselves as successful.

Structuring schools to support development

The SDP framework helps redesign school operations based on guiding principles that promote respect. Using the metaphor of a schoolhouse, Figure 1.2 shows how the various elements of the SDP work together. Strong relationships supporting child/adolescent growth along the six developmental pathways are the foundation of this schoolhouse, from which a supportive school can emerge in an atmosphere of collegiality, with a deep understanding of how children learn and develop.

Three operations guide the work happening in classrooms, hallways, offices, and the cafeteria: (1) the Comprehensive School Plan, which includes social and academic components; (2) staff development; and (3) a process of assessment regarding what's working and what needs modification in the course of continuous improvement. Guided by the School Planning and Management Team, the Parent Team, and the Student and Staff Support Team, the leadership and operations of the school are distributed among a key set of stakeholders. Parents, teachers, students, and staff all have a voice and collectively take responsibility for decision making, reflection, ongoing data analysis, and course correction when necessary.

Finally, through a spirit and expectation of collaboration, consensus decision making, and a no-fault approach to problem solving, the roof of the schoolhouse is in place. These guiding principles act as a cover, protecting the school from discouragement when setbacks occur. Even as the process of change brings tumultuous

FIGURE 1.2 | Model of the SDP Process

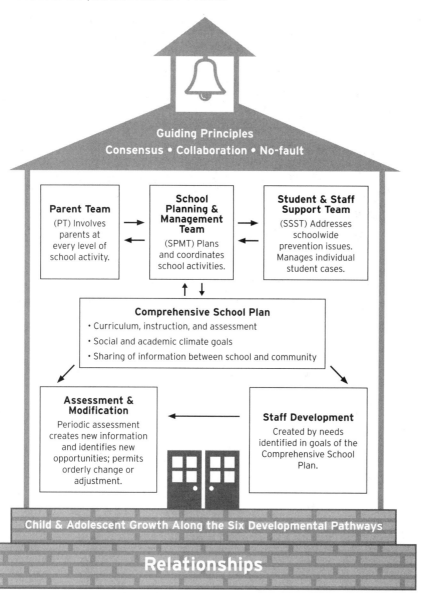

Source: From Yale Child Study Center, School Development Program. Copyright 1998 by Yale Child Study Center. Adapted with permission.

weather—driving rain, penetrating sun, and relentless wind—the adults who have committed to focused change will, over time and with an overarching belief in mutual respect and teamwork, persist despite challenges and barriers that will certainly arise.

In this model, the school is viewed as a system whose purpose is to provide a supportive, warm, and caring climate within which relationships are nurtured and valued. In this way, the environment itself perpetuates a way of being that changes behavior, supports children's development, and facilitates deep and meaningful learning.

This framework was developed over time as members of the Yale Child Study Center team spent time in schools figuring out what children and adults needed to create a strong, supportive climate. As Comer explained in a 2017 interview,

> From the beginning, [we had to] throw out the notion that we knew what children needed. We had to learn what schools were doing and look at outcomes and see whether they were meeting the developmental needs of children. We realized teachers and administrators at that time in the '60s and '70s weren't receiving preparation [related to] child and adolescent development principles. That's what we did—tried to create culture within school that allowed adults and caretakers to have some understanding of how development and academic learning were inextricably linked. [We] focus[ed] on how to create culture—figured that was critical—for everybody to keep focus on how children develop.

The School Development Program operates from an understanding that just as child development is holistic and consists of many parts working together, the school system or ecology consists of many interrelated components that must work together to support children's development and learning. A strengths-based approach sees the potential at every level, from the child to adults and the broader milieu. Although schools cannot replace the family, they can recognize and draw out the positive health and social ingredients that are potentially and actively present in each family, cultural, and social setting (Cohen & Solnit, 1996).

The use of data as a guide in a systematic evaluation process drives decisions about how to support children's development and learning. School teams come together to pore over school records on behavior, attendance, performance, and other matters to understand how children are developing along the six pathways and where intervention is needed. The framework also recognizes the centrality of teachers and teacher preparation in upholding and carrying out the framework.

Comer's framework of child development is built on several truths about human behavior. Individuals need community and support to develop; behavior is a reaction to one's perceptions of the environment; thus, to change an individual's behavior, one must understand the individual's perceptions, attitudes, feelings, and abilities (Comer, Haynes, Joyner, & Ben-Avie, 1996). As adults in schools watch and listen to children more attentively, in light of what they are learning about child development, they are able to create new environments that are more supportive, positive, engaging, and child-centered. When this occurs, it stands to reason—and evidence shows—that development along the pathways improves as well.

A Whole Child Approach to Education

Long before most educators began talking about "whole child" approaches to education, the School Development Program invented such an approach. According to ASCD (www.ascd.org/whole-child.aspx), the goals of a whole child approach are that

1. Each student enters school healthy and learns about and practices a healthy lifestyle.

2. Each student learns in an environment that is physically and emotionally safe for students and adults.
3. Each student is actively engaged in learning and is connected to the school and broader community.
4. Each student has access to personalized learning and is supported by qualified, caring adults.
5. Each student is challenged academically and prepared for success in college or further study and for employment and participation in a global environment.

A whole child approach seeks to address the distinctive strengths, needs, and interests of students as they engage in learning. It recognizes the importance of and interrelationships among all areas of development and designs school policies and practices to support them. These include access to nutritious food, health care, and social supports; access to strong relationships; educative and restorative disciplinary practices; and learning opportunities that are designed to activate and engage students, while supporting their motivation and self-confidence to persevere and succeed. All aspects of children's being are supported in an effort to ensure that learning happens in deep, meaningful, and lasting ways.

To achieve these goals, educators must understand how developmental processes unfold over time and interact in different contexts so that they can design supportive environments. Although development follows general trends, the processes of development unfold differently for each child, influenced by the interaction between unique aspects of the child and the child's family, community, and classroom contexts. As a result, schools must be designed to attend to the unique needs and trajectories of individual children as well as to support patterns of development, and educators must know how to differentiate instruction and supports to enable optimal growth in competence, confidence, and motivation.

The Science of Learning and Development

The Comer School Development Program offers a model for "rallying the whole village" in the service of all aspects of student development and learning. It is built on decades of accumulated knowledge about how children grow and develop that has been reinforced by new research from the biological sciences and neurosciences, as well as the learning sciences.

Recent research demonstrates how cognitive development and social-emotional development are tightly interrelated and how social-emotional development can bolster academic learning and performance. It also demonstrates how risks are heightened for children who experience adversity and trauma, which disproportionately affect those who live in poverty. Recent syntheses of this research (Cantor et al., 2018; Olson, 2017; Osher et al., 2018) confirm the following:

1. Development is malleable. Children learn new skills from birth through adulthood because the brain never stops growing and changing in response to experiences and relationships. The nature of these experiences and relationships matters greatly to the growth of the brain and the development of skills. The wiring of important neural circuits is enhanced by good nutrition; positive, affirming interactions and responses; experiences that support a sense of safety and trust that enables attachment; and experiences that allow for exploration of language and the physical world, with rich materials that allow children to inquire into the world around them. Development occurs within concentric circles of influence, beginning with the family and extending to the school, the community, and larger economic and social forces that influence children's development directly and indirectly.

2. Human development is variable. The pace and profile of each child's development is unique. Although development generally progresses in somewhat predictable stages, children begin at differ-ent starting points and learn and acquire skills at different rates and in different ways. This variability means that schools should avoid labeling children or designing learning experiences around a myth-ical average. When they try to force all children to fit one sequence or pacing guide, they miss the opportunity to nurture the individual potential of every child, and they can cause children (as well as teach-ers) to adopt counterproductive views about themselves and their own learning potential that undermine progress. Rather than assum-ing all children will respond to the same teaching approaches equally well, teachers must differentiate and personalize supports and inter-vention for different children.

3. Human relationships are the essential ingredient that cat-alyzes healthy development and learning. Supportive, responsive relationships with caring adults are the foundation for healthy devel-opment and learning. Brain architecture is developed by the presence of warm, consistent, attuned relationships; positive experiences; and positive perceptions of these experiences (Center on the Developing Child at Harvard University, 2016). For example, a mother's ability to accurately interpret and respond to her infant's cues affects the wiring of brain circuits that support later skills. The same wiring can occur when teachers and peers respond in supportive ways. When teachers are responsive and affirming, children's development and learning are enhanced. The role of relationships in childhood and adolescence also has an important protective effect. Research has found that when children have a stable relationship with at least one committed adult, this relationship can buffer the potentially negative effects of even serious adversity. Children benefit when relationships are consistent, empathetic, responsive to their needs, and model pro-ductive social, emotional, and academic behaviors, thereby building developmentally appropriate skills.

4. Adversity affects learning—and the way schools respond matters. Stress is a normal part of life, but excessive stress can throw learning and development off track and undermine children's well-being. School practices can either exacerbate or buffer the effects of childhood adversity. When threatened, humans activate a stress-response system, which includes a surge in hormones (cortisol and adrenaline) that make them focused, vigilant, and alert until it is appropriate to return to a calmer state. But prolonged stress caused by ongoing adversity damages the functioning of bodily organs and creates anxiety and depression, also interfering with executive functioning and memory.

Traumatic events can occur both outside and inside schools. In schools where students encounter implicit bias and stereotyping or punitive discipline tactics rather than supports for handling adversity, their stress is doubled. Punitive school responses often include exclusion through suspensions and expulsions, which disproportionately affect low-income students of color and students with disabilities, who receive harsher penalties than other students who engage in similar behaviors (Cardichon & Darling-Hammond, 2017).

However, schools, families, and communities can buffer the effects of stress by facilitating supportive adult-child relationships that extend over time; teaching and reinforcing social-emotional skills that help children handle adversity, such as the ability to calm emotions and manage responses; and creating strong, dependable, supportive routines for both managing classrooms and checking in on student needs (Center on the Developing Child at Harvard University, 2016).

5. Learning is social, emotional, and academic. Emotions and social relationships affect learning. Positive relationships, including a trusting relationship with a teacher, and positive emotions, including interest and excitement, open up the mind to learning. Negative emotions, including fear of failure, anxiety, and self-doubt, reduce the capacity of the brain to process information and to learn. A child's best performance occurs under conditions of high support and low threat.

In addition, children's abilities to manage their emotions influence learning. For example, learning to calm oneself and focus attention provide the foundation for learning, including the ability to persist with hard tasks and to pursue interests over a longer period of time. Students' interpersonal skills, including their ability to interact positively with peers and adults, to resolve conflicts, and to work in teams, all contribute to effective learning. Students' motivation and their "metacognitive skills," the ability to guide their own learning and understanding, also are important for effective learning.

Students who have a growth mindset—that is, they believe they can improve through effort, trying new strategies, and seeking help—are less likely to become discouraged and more likely to try harder after encountering difficulties. They are more likely to tackle tasks at the edge of their current skillset than students who believe their intelligence is fixed. This mindset translates into stronger performance in school and in other tasks in life as well. These skills, which help children modulate stress, develop more advanced skills, and productively engage in learning and in life, can be taught.

Engagement and effort are supported in classrooms where children feel they are not typecast or stereotyped, where they see that they can improve with effort (for example, by revising their work), where they are respected and valued by their teachers and peers, and where they are working on things that matter to themselves and others.

Creating a Positive School Climate[1]

Given that emotions and relationships strongly influence learning—and these are the by-products of how students are treated at schools, as well as at home and in their communities—a positive school climate is at the core of a successful educational experience. Children learn when they feel safe and supported, and their learning is

---

[1] This section draws in part on Melnick, Cook-Harvey, & Darling-Hammond, 2017.

impaired when they are fearful, traumatized, or overcome with emotion (National Scientific Council on the Developing Child, 2010). Thus, they need both supportive environments and well-developed abilities to manage stress and to cope with the inevitable conflicts and frustrations of school and life beyond school. As Comer noted,

> In order to provide our children and youth with a more "science-of-learning-and-development-aligned" education, what's needed most of all is a mindset that stops arguing that there are smart and dumb kids—good and bad kids. All kids are differently developed and underdeveloped. [Schools should be created so that] all of the people a child comes into contact with and structures and procedures are designed to support kids, so they can be successful in any situation, academic in particular, and so they can be successful in life.

It is important that schools provide a positive learning environment that includes security and support that maximize students' ability to learn social and emotional skills as well as academic content. A positive school climate "is based on patterns of students', parents' and school personnel's experience of school life; it also reflects norms, goals, values, interpersonal relationships, teaching and learning practices, and organizational structures" (National School Climate Center, n.d.).

The National School Climate Center outlines 13 dimensions that cover all aspects of the school environment, ranging from physical and emotional safety and the physical maintenance of the school building and grounds to relationships, engagement, and a sense of belonging. Many of these constructs can also be considered "conditions for learning," which enable the development of students' social and emotional skills. For example, students need social supports from adults and peers that make them feel connected to the school before they can develop optimism or a growth mindset. Similarly, students need to feel safe from verbal abuse and bullying in order to develop strong social awareness and relationship skills.

A recent report reviewed 78 school-climate studies published since 2000 and found that a positive school climate can mitigate the negative effects of poverty on academic achievement (Berkowitz, Moore, Astor, & Benbenishty, 2016). The authors conclude that "a more positive school climate is related to improved academic achievement, beyond the expected level of achievement based on student and school socio-economic status backgrounds" (p. 34). The most important elements of school climate contributing to increased achievement were associated with teacher-student relationships, including aspects such as warmth, acceptance, and teacher support.

School climate describes how students, teachers, and parents respond to school culture. Culture, in turn, refers to a school's set of norms, beliefs, and practices, and it is driven by the school's values and expectations that are "embedded in structures and practices and transmitted explicitly and implicitly" (Jones & Bouffard, 2012). Together, culture and climate set the tone at a school and can be seen in the physical environment, experienced during the learning process, and felt in how people within the school interact with one another (Melnick et al., 2017). As students and school personnel refine their social and emotional competence, school climate improves; likewise, a positive school climate creates the atmosphere within which social and emotional learning can take place (Jennings & Greenberg, 2009).

Although climate and culture are palpable influences in a school, the structures and practices that build them are almost invisible to outsiders. As Comer once remarked,

> Often over the years people can't figure out [what caused the change in schools we worked in]. They know something good has happened because of attitudes and behaviors—but they can't figure out how it happened. In other settings,

these same kids would be acting out in troublesome ways. A reporter [who] came and spent the week [at one of our schools] said, "This is a good school, but I don't know why." It's built into the structures and processes that create change in people—in their attitudes, beliefs, ways—that enable them to get along and support development of kids, rather than controlling kids through punishment, which sets up negative behaviors. We give kids knowledge, experience, and relationship skills that enable them to succeed in a school setting. [That approach] decreases and prevents behavior problems and increases their desire to perform and be successful. But you can miss the effect or impact of structures and processes if you don't understand how they all come together to create culture.

Creating a Whole Child Balance

Many educators have noted that the policy climate during the No Child Left Behind era created disincentives to taking this broader context into account. Instead, the focus of schooling largely shifted to sanctions and punishments, competition and comparison, as these were attached to test scores that were expected to climb higher year after year. Schools with low scores—often those serving high proportions of students of color and those living in poverty—could be placed in mandated interventions, often without the necessary resources to achieve different results, or they could be reconstituted or closed.

Accountability policies created incentives for schools to push out their most academically and socially challenging students so as to boost scores, placing their most marginalized students at even more risk (Wald & Losen, 2003). Zero-tolerance discipline policies pushed many out, while a narrowed, test-prep curriculum that focused on low-quality tests caused others to disengage (Ladd, 2001). Labeling schools serving high-needs students as failing, and instituting sanctions against them, also caused well-qualified educators to flee these schools, leaving the students, quite often, with a revolving door of underprepared, overwhelmed novice teachers even less able to create a stable, caring, engaging learning environment.

Lester Young Jr., superintendent of Brooklyn's Community School District 13 from 1993 until 2003, described how the district's implementation of the Comer Process shifted the focus of schooling in his district during the era of high-stakes testing. Young characterized the process of transformation provided by the SDP as "the glue" that brought the adults at the school and district level together in a focused, collaborative way to "change the culture of a system in support of the students" (personal communication, January 2, 2018). Young explained how going through the Comer Process for school reform required the adults—parents, teachers, leaders—to shift their paradigm, revising the rationale for how and why schooling happens for children:

> We made a strategic point of focusing on the idea that it's development that supports learning, and not the other way around. This was right around the time when people were starting to get very much focused on high-stakes testing; so people felt, OK, well, if the kid gets high scores and does well, then he'll do better. And what we said very simply is that you've got to be concerned with all the areas of development because they're all connected. What we felt very strongly is that our goal as the adults is try to figure out as many ways as we could to assure that youngsters were successful in school. . . . So we had to make sure that we were attuned to the physical development of kids, the linguistic development, the social, emotional, psychological. We understood that all of these things were related to cognitive development, and if youngsters are not doing well academically and your only focus is on academics, then you

spend most of your time chasing a score. We never felt that was an education.

Mary Mayrick, districtwide SDP facilitator in 2001 in Westbury, New York, also pointed to the importance of seeing the child as a whole rather than just focusing on raising scores:

> I think when you're not only trying to service that cognitive slice, when your intention is to make sure that we're balancing with the other developmental pathways, it's a different way of offering information to the kids. . . . The intention to hold space for them to grow as a whole child is completely different than the intention of getting their brain to be able to function to accept all this information and then to be able to spit it out in a way that's not developmentally appropriate.

Mayrick went on to explain how using the lens of the developmental pathways in turn had an impact on all aspects of the school environment and the discourse surrounding the work of teaching and learning: "It changed our conversation; it changed how we talked about the students; it even changed sometimes how we looked at ourselves."

To bring out the best in children, adults must interact collaboratively and sensitively with one another. To implement the Comer Process at a high level requires that adults do the following:

- Behave collaboratively, modeling productive problem solving.
- Demonstrate flexibility and expertise in change management.
- Relate knowledge of child and youth development to student learning.
- Make decisions that are in the best interests of children. (Comer et al., 2004)

This approach allows teachers to see students' potential, encourage their imagination, and recognize special gifts that the children and their families may not yet be aware of. This hopefulness can become internalized by students when there is mutual trust and ongoing opportunity for meaningful teaching and learning. As children are socialized in a caring school community, they develop increasing capacity to act as effective agents of change (Cohen & Solnit, 1996).

The Comer Process has an intentionality that lends itself to satisfying and lasting change. Unlike other reforms that have faded as people grew weary and slowly stopped implementation, or those reforms that lived solely within the vision of one leader, implementing the Comer Process means changing the lifeblood of the school itself—transforming the environment, the knowledge base of and interactions among adults and children, and the mode of operation—so much so that reverting to old habits is very difficult. The SDP encourages a "knowledge adoption" mindset rather than a "program adoption" mindset. The aim is to infuse developmental knowledge into education with structures that provide a means to do so. Ultimately, the work is about promoting the development of children, training and supporting adults so that they can support students, and designing schools so that they can support adults and children.

A productive school grounded in an understanding of the science of learning and development keeps students in school and promotes academic results by way of meaningful, deep learning, and helps students acquire the social-emotional skills, habits, and mindsets necessary to be successful in school and in life beyond school. In a sense, the SDP school is a training academy for the rest of life. When an SDP school is working well, it is a model of a just society (Comer et al., 2004). The conditions of the school can be created to bring out that which is good, helpful, and supportive in each person.

2

The School Development Program: Design and Outcomes

Our intervention program was not based on a single theory of human, institutional, or system behavior. In fact, one of the problems in intervention research in schools is that there is no theory broad enough and specific enough to be very helpful. Our approach was to bring our knowledge of the various theories of human and institutional behavior to the school setting, learn about the school, apply the principles of the social and behavioral sciences that appeared most helpful, and in the process elaborate a theory of intervention specific to our program, with principles applicable to school intervention across the society.

–James P. Comer, **School Power: Implications of an Intervention Project**

There was a time when schools were part of a network of community-centered institutions, where parents and teachers lived side by side and worked together to wrap themselves around students as partners in ushering children through adolescence and into adulthood, where those young adults would become active members of the same community that helped to raise them. Although this ideal still exists in some places in the United States, such congruence and connection between home and school is no longer the norm.

So as schools and families have increasingly separated themselves from one another, as the dynamics of our society have become more independent and less communal, and as the expectation of schools has shifted to one in which they are seen as a predominantly academic enterprise, the focus on children's healthy development has taken a backseat to reading, writing, and arithmetic. And this shift has come with a cost.

The pressures of pacing guides, the standardization of curriculum and assessments, and the impersonal nature of the factory model of school has further distanced students, teachers, and parents from one another. The School Development Program offers a process whereby schools can restore eroded relationships or build them where none existed before.

The Nine-Part Model: Teams, Operations, and Principles

The School Development Program is a way to help place child development at the center of all decisions. It is not a cookie-cutter program defined by a set of procedures. However, as Comer and his colleagues from Yale sought to help schools focus on development, they realized that structures can be enabling for the school development process, so they created vehicles by which adults could learn, collaborate, make decisions, and continuously improve their strategies for supporting children.

In 1968–69, the first year of the School Development Program, parents and staff members at the Baldwin and King schools joined with the Yale team to develop a nine-part process to rectify previously ineffective and damaging interactions and to guide the school improvement work moving forward. As noted in Chapter 1, these nine components are three *mechanisms*, three *operations*, and three guiding *principles*. The mechanisms are the "who" of the program, or the three teams: the School Planning and Management Team (SPMT), the Student and Staff Support Team (SSST), and the Parent Team. The three operations are the "what" of the program: the Comprehensive School Plan, staff development, and assessment and modification. Finally, the three principles are the "how" of the program—consensus, collaboration, and no-fault problem solving—which dictate how people within the teams and the school overall will work together.

Teams for planning and supporting student learning[1]

In *Transforming School Leadership and Management to Support Student Learning and Development*, the SDP is described as a "structure as well as a process for mobilizing adults" that "replaces traditional organization" (Joyner, Ben-Avie, & Comer, 2004, p. 18). The *mechanisms*, or teams, are the central bodies within which the main work of the adults gets done. These teams drive the reform process by designing a plan, testing it, reflecting on progress, and refining next steps based on data. Joyner and colleagues (2004, p. 18) describe the teams as follows:

- **School Planning and Management Team:** The SPMT develops a comprehensive school plan; sets academic, social, and community relationship goals; and coordinates all school activities, including staff development programs. The team creates critical dialogue around teaching and learning and monitors progress to identify needed adjustments to the school plan as well as opportunities to support the plan. Members of the team include administrators, teachers, support staff, and parents.

- **The Student and Staff Support Team:** The SSST promotes desirable social conditions and relationships. It connects all of the school's student services, facilitates the sharing of information and advice, addresses individual student needs, accesses resources outside the school, and develops prevention programs. Membership includes individuals in the school community who possess specialized knowledge,

---

[1]This section draws in part from E. T. Joyner, M. Ben-Avie, and J. P. Comer, *Transforming School Leadership and Management to Support Student Learning and Development: The Field Guide to Comer Schools in Action*, 2004, Corwin Press, p. 18.

training, or expertise in mental health or child and adolescent development theory and practice.

- **Parent Team:** PT involves parents in the school by developing activities through which the parents can support the school's social and academic programs. Composed of parents, this team also selects representatives to serve on the School Planning and Management Team.

Shelley Leppert reflected on the importance of the team structure during her time as district SDP facilitator in Paterson, New Jersey:

> Weekly cluster meetings helped the children academically because then everyone at these weekly meetings had a finger on the pulse of how the students were doing. If they were having difficulty with another subject area or another faculty member, perhaps another member of the team could give insight. Everyone was in the know; everyone was in the loop. There weren't just a few people that knew what was happening in the building. We tried to keep those lines of communication open all the time.... So there really was that family feeling that was built, [in] the famous words of James Comer, it takes a village. In fact, it did. We were a village.

Operations for doing the work

The decision-making bodies mentioned in the previous section are responsible for ensuring that the three *operations* of the school are functional. The first operation is the *Comprehensive School Plan*, which, much like a company's strategic plan, is an overarching, guiding document that "gives direction and specific focus to the school improvement process" and articulates specific goals, activities, action steps, and strategies to address the academic, social, behavioral, and relational aspects of the school itself (Comer et al., 1996, p. 13).

The School Planning and Management Team uses multiple sources of data to inform and revise the plan as necessary. Sheila Brantley, former teacher and then SDP district facilitator in New Haven, described the use of data to inform practice as the most obvious and important aspect of the Comer process of transformation. She explained that traditionally, in schools that operate without the developmental approach that the SDP provides, "a child would be discussed because of behavior but without the evidence backing it up." By contrast, in the SDP approach, teams look at "frequency, triggers, relationships with family, with teacher, with peers . . . [and] use the data, and developmental attachment theory, and knowledge of social emotional learning to do action planning, identify who is accountable, who is responsible for what, decide on when is the next meeting . . . [it is] not just complaining about the kids."

Building the capacity of educators to approach reforming school environments with this lens requires a shift in paradigm: moving from an understanding of theory to knowing how that theory translates to practice is the result of intentional, focused, and personalized *professional development*—the second operaton of the SDP. For many educators, learning how to think diagnostically about the many ways that children are developing is a departure from how many teachers and leaders are trained in preservice preparation programs. Brantley explained this challenge more fully:

> We spend many hours teaching teachers how to analyze. [When we had] teams that were doing well, that were effective, we welcomed others to come watch and sit in on how it was done. SDP did training after training. It wasn't just one conference for the year. [For] any school that needed anything, we would go into the school and train there, and go in the classroom and model how to use developmental pathways in the classroom. People understood the theory

but didn't know how to apply it on an everyday basis, so we showed them how to put it into lesson plans and how to consider the cognitive and linguistic and emotional aspects of development into the lessons. And we gave them templates, materials, anything. When we gathered good information [from one school], we would come back and disperse it to all the schools.

The Comprehensive School Plan provides guidance on how and what educators will need to learn—skills, strategies, and tools—as well as a process by which to evaluate the effectiveness of pedagogies. With guidance from the SPMT, "teachers become alert to their own professional development needs and take the lead in designing their own continuing education" (Comer et al., 1996, p. 21).

Finally, the SDP model of school reform is iterative, with a focus on data-informed continuous improvement. In many ways, the change process is alive—ever reflecting, analyzing, and evolving based on the needs of the children and the outcomes that are generated. This *assessment and modification* process is the last of the three school operations within the Comer methodology. The process "generates useful data on program processes and outcomes, feeds back information to inform program modification where necessary, and establishes new goals and objectives" (Comer et al., 1996, p. 14).

It's important to note that data in the SDP is more than test scores. In the Comer Process, faculty and staff become equipped to gather evidence from a host of sources: observations of students and teachers in classrooms, concerns and input from parents, discussions among colleagues as they problem-solve around how to support individuals or groups of students, discipline and attendance data, and more. As schools use a wide range of data, educators become better able to holistically assess the needs, challenges, and barriers impeding student learning and development. This approach allows staff to think more broadly about different strategies and solutions that can be implemented or adapted to meet those identified needs. When test scores are the only data source, the range of possible sources and solutions is often narrowed, and the bulk of the onus is on students and their deficiencies. However, when a school is willing and able to step back and assess the range of influences on students—family, community, school structures, policies, pedagogies, curriculum—the school becomes better able to identify the root of the problem and determine where to make changes that will address the real issue.

Lester Young Jr., former superintendent of Brooklyn's District 13, brought together the various teams from his schools for annual retreats as a way to "summarize what happened the year before and to lay out what the priorities were for the coming year, which included what our targets, our goals, our expectations were." He explained:

> And then we spent the rest of that time strategizing around what had to happen in each individual school to realize those goals and objectives. . . . There were opportunities for people to talk specifically about what they needed to do in their schools—to examine the data for their schools and to put in place a set of goals and objectives. But all of that was in the context of where we were going as a district. So it was really used as a kind of unifying force. It was great because [for many of us] it was the first time that people could not only focus on their individual schools, but they could also see how what was going on in their schools contributed to the growth of the district.

This continual reflection and process of asking critical questions is applied before, during, and at the end of every change process. This practice anchors the school community to the bigger vision even when absorbed in minute details. It also emphasizes the positive while acknowledging room for improvement.

Principles

To achieve this kind of school change requires adults to work in new ways to achieve a new environment within which children will learn and develop. Chaotic or dysfunctional schools often display a measure of distrust and dislike among the stakeholders. The guiding SDP *principles*—consensus, collaboration, and no-fault problem solving—were developed as "relationship guidelines" by which people could work together to motivate the creation of a positive school climate (Comer & Emmons, 2006).

Consensus

As the school community begins to practice decision making and interacting using the SDP principles, relationships can be strengthened and repaired. The principles provide a procedure by which members of the school community learn to interact with one another and review their aims and methods to identify problems in a no-fault atmosphere. In short, the guiding principles "permit the development and implementation of creative ways of dealing with problems, using the collective good judgment . . . of school staff and parents" (Comer et al., 1996, p. 10).

At the heart of the SDP is community building. All of the activities of the SDP revolve around building and strengthening a sense of community (Comer et al., 1996). The processes involving collaboration, no-fault problem solving, and decision making by consensus permeate all aspects of the program, including professional development. The experiences of a new SDP project manager making his first presentation to educators underscores this point. The project manager had prepared thoroughly and presented each element in detail. When he asked for feedback on his presentation, Comer gently replied, "You did a great job, Jack," and then paused before adding, "but you missed the whole point. In every interaction you are either building community or breaking community. The mechanisms are secondary" (Comer et al., 1996, p. 148).

The SDP values the principles and processes as means of building community that are infused into all aspects of the work. The guiding principles, which hold all adults involved accountable for modeling collaboration, no-fault problem solving, and reaching consensus in each activity, create relationships and common ground that allow adults to work more productively together.

Consensus decision making is a departure from voter-based decision making. Voting produces winners and losers, and there is a risk that "losers" may feel that they have no stake in the final decision because they voted differently. Consensus therefore allows for "brainstorming, in-depth discussion, cross-fertilization of ideas and a plan for trying different solutions in some sequence" (Comer et al., 1996, p. 9). Arriving at a consensus decision, then, is the result of a respectful process that includes gathering all individual opinions, discussing, evaluating, and choosing among those ideas collectively (Lunenburg, 2011).

Ruth Baskerville, principal at Norman S. Weir School in Paterson, New Jersey, from 1997 to 2004, explained how the healthy collaboration and consensus decision making worked to create staff synergy and momentum in turning around the school:

> Consensus was a big deal; we did everything by consensus—everything. And most of the time, if I didn't like an idea but the consensus was going that way, I went that way, you know, and people just bought in. The idea of consensus was important because it meant if my idea is not at the top of the list this time, it may come up next time; so there was always fluidity, and that, of course, bred the collaboration. So collaboration was big. There were no people on an island; we were all in it together, and we just felt that. So we had these committees; we had respective chairs; we sent ideas to the management team; we had a steady flow of info from the top (me), to the child, all the way down. There was

healthy dialogue among all stakeholders. We valued what the secretary said, the cafeteria staff said; we valued the custodians—they had insight—and so that was good. And my facilitator, Shelley Leppert, was invaluable because many times teachers would go to her first, just because she wasn't the principal. We had a great rapport; so that way she would say, well, there's something brewing over here, or we have a little weak link over here, we have too many new teachers in, you know, 1st grade, or something. And she was like my troubleshooter, so I could empower the next group to be creative thinkers. I loved that everybody was unafraid of failure, [and] I just wasn't threatened by subordinates. I embraced the idea.

Collaboration

Productive *collaboration* requires those involved to have a sense of shared and mutual goals and a willingness to each contribute based on strengths and talents. Also crucial for collaboration is openness to share ideas, try different strategies, and come back to the drawing board to reflect and make changes based on what has worked or hasn't worked. When applying this principle to school transformation and improvement, collaboration is critical. Unlike the situation in many schools, where siloed, individual work is pervasive, collaboration engenders sharing and communication. Furthermore, as schools can be political and potentially rife with competing agendas, collaboration that does not paralyze the principal—or any other individual—requires respect for other points of view and a willingness to work as part of a team (Haynes & Comer, 1993).

This type of respectful collaboration does not come about overnight; instead it requires intentional culture building among all stakeholders—especially for those educators and staff in the schools every day, working with children. Many SDP participants reflected about the need to provide opportunities for the adults to see one another not only as colleagues but also as teammates. Mary Mayrick explained how as SDP district facilitator in Westbury Public Schools in New York she would always allow for "even the smallest amount of time for some relationship building and team building, [which was] really vital to the process."

No-fault problem solving

As people are working together to make decisions and achieve stated goals, there will be problems along the way that require teams to surface and address problems as they arise. Doing so requires a certain amount of trust and vulnerability to ensure that people don't feel blamed or judged for challenges, mistakes, and problems. *No-fault problem solving* "helps teams focus on creating workable, effective solutions that serve the best interest of students" (Lunenburg, 2011, p. 8). Having a no-fault approach lays the foundation for brainstorming ideas and solutions where all team members are "in it together"; in this way, then, "everyone accepts equal responsibility for change" (Comer et al., 1996, p. 10).

Mary Mayrick spoke highly of the importance of using specific strategies to instill the principles and change the way in which adults communicated with one another in meetings. She reflected that as the district facilitator, she was in many ways like a "pusher," insisting that meetings had a "sound structure" while allowing participants to have a "voice, but not the voice that's going to blame or defend." This distinction becomes really important for schools that are in the process of trying to find their way out of negative habits built on distrust for colleagues and administrators. Mayrick explained, "In some of the schools, the culture was a little bit more challenging, but I never traveled without my set of table cards with the guiding principles, with the roles, and I went to every school and always had an extra set if I needed to leave them. . . . [I] really tried to model how much that worked, [and it was] the same structures that we would use with the kids."

This no-fault approach not only dictates how adults in the SDP schools work together but also trickles down to students in intentional ways. Ruth Baskerville explained how this approach changed how and where learning took place in her school:

> There was simply no fault, and we let the kids feel that too—that to get something incorrect was not a punishment, a negative.... From the child all the way to the parents, we stressed no-fault. Risk taking was encouraged. It wasn't punished. So we had vibrant committees. The people who became the chairs—and the chairs rotated—they brought ideas to the management team . . . nothing was off limits. [For example,] someone had a great idea to work outside. We were a school in the middle of an urban city, and our school emptied out onto the sidewalk, so we really didn't have a playground at all. But what we were able to do, we could walk the block, and there was nature outside, and so there was a way to do a lesson under a tree for the kindergartners or the 1st graders, . . . we could do some of those kinds of things.

Together, these principles inspire new ideas, provide a protocol for making decisions, and offer a safe climate within which problems can be addressed. There is a cohesion then among the school community as a whole, as the cycle of reflecting, adapting, and growing becomes the dominant mode of operation and the momentum of forward progress remains steady.

Evolution of the School Development Program

The SDP approach evolved with ongoing learning. In the summer after the first year of the program, when Baldwin and King elementary schools were still struggling, the Yale staff and the New Haven staff came together to brainstorm, decide upon, and implement a host of organizational and managerial changes. In his book *School Power* (1980, pp. 101–104), Comer articulated some of these major changes:

- Hiring a school district coordinator who would work full-time for the implementation of the program.
- Reviving the parent committee and taking significant feedback from parents about the responsibilities and input they would offer the school.
- Improving communication between the schools and the school district regarding what, how, and why the program staff and school faculty were making decisions and to update on progress.
- Redesigning the role of social workers so that, instead of a traditional case load approach, the social workers could train teachers and staff on how to carry out specific tasks, interventions, and programs.
- Designing and implementing workshop sessions for teachers on curriculum design, engaging and communicating with parents, progress reports, finding student assets rather than deficits, child behavior, strategies to reduce anxiety, and educative, goal-oriented behavior management rather than the use of consequential or punitive measures.

These approaches ultimately became program elements that carried forward into the overall design. With grants from the Ford Foundation, the New Prospect Foundation, and Title 1 funds from the New Haven School System, the Baldwin-King Program—named after the two initial schools, Susan E. Baldwin and Dr. Martin Luther King Jr. elementary schools—became part of the Ford Foundation's broader national effort to leverage resources in support of university and public school partnerships. In the first decade of the program, or the Pilot Stage, the project team viewed the intervention process as a research and development effort, a period to test the theory and draw implications for national school contexts struggling with many of the same issues (Comer, 1980).

As the success of the SDP in the two elementary schools in New Haven became better known, more schools adopted this model as a process of reform. In the Field Testing Stage, from 1978 to 1987, staff from Yale began using a direct service approach to inform, train, and support districts and schools that were part of this emerging SDP network. The focus during this period was to refine and test the replicability of the intervention in New Haven. By the mid-1980s, the SDP adopted a train-the-trainer model in which teams of educators and parents were trained in workshops at the Yale Child Study Center so that they could return to their home districts and implement the strategies with fidelity. This period also marked the start of a robust research and evaluation agenda to determine the SDP's impact on academic achievement, attendance, behavior, self-concept, perceptions of school and classroom climate, and social competence (Comer et al., 1996).

Beginning in 1988, the program expanded rapidly, with the help of a grant from the Rockefeller Foundation. This grant supported a Dissemination stage in which an expanded train-the-trainer model allowed districts across the country to implement the SDP process. After working for a decade with the two schools in New Haven (1968–1978) and with three districts in the decade thereafter (1978–1987), the program rapidly expanded to 650 schools in 80 school districts in 21 states and the District of Columbia by 1997. As of today, it has reached more than 1,000 schools in the United States and abroad.

Strategies for Supporting School Transformation

Achieving school transformation via the School Development Program is a multifaceted process, requiring many different elements to work simultaneously and in coordination with one another. As schools began embarking on the SDP reform process, Yale and SDP central staff played a key role in helping schools and districts fully integrate the nine elements of the program.

Diagnosing school assets and needs

Just as the SDP sees students through a positive, no-fault lens as developing human beings with assets to be supported and needs to be addressed, so it considers schools as places with assets and needs that should be supported in their development. As Fay Brown, director of child and adolescent development at the School Development Program, explains,

> When we start working with a school, the first thing we do is what we call a contextual analysis, where we go into the school and meet with different groups so we can learn from them what's working well along several dimensions in the school, several factors of school functioning—like the leadership of the school, student development, academic achievement of the students, parent engagement in the school, communication levels in the school, the different structures that are in the school, the district support that the school gets, and so forth. We give them a list with about 15 different factors that can either impede or foster school functioning, and we ask them to look at the list and talk to us about what's working well on all or any of these factors. [We also ask,] "What's not working so well, so that you can get our support and improve in these areas?" We spend about an hour or so with each of the teams that are set up for us to meet. We might end up being in the school for six or seven hours to get information from the school.
>
> After examining our notes, we create a report, then set up an appointment to go back and share with the administrator and his/her leadership team what we found through the contextual analysis. Then with their input, we co-construct a plan as to how we are going to work with the school.

This process illustrates how the SDP is not a standardized or scripted approach. It is a process of helping a school examine how to align its own development with the development of children.

To help a school improve its climate and culture takes tremendous work from both the school and the district. This process requires a bottom-up appetite for change that is supported through complementary district initiatives and adequate resources allocated in response to school-based needs. *Leadership, vision,* and *resources* must be coordinated and aligned; if there is anything less than 100 percent buy-in from school and district staff, the change process will be ineffective, will stagnate, and will eventually fail.

Organizing professional development

Professional development is essential during school transformation, as adults are learning and growing as professionals and as people, moving from an individualistic mindset to a collective, growth-oriented mindset as they are embedded in teams. Such a shift requires that capacity-building activities be developmentally appropriate, personalized, and applicable to the daily work of educators and staff in the school. To support these changes, the Yale SDP staff provided critical professional development support to district and school leaders, teachers, and parents, often during summer "Comer conferences" in Connecticut to which people from around the United States traveled. As the program expanded, train-the-trainer workshops were held in various locations to allow educators to take information back to their respective schools and districts.

The SDP facilitator position, or "the SDP change agent in the field," is responsible for ensuring that the teams are working together in a true collaborative spirit. This individual might assign roles during meetings, build an agenda, and make sure that all voices are heard. The facilitator maintains a focus on the children rather than the concerns of the adults. As the school teams become autonomous and cooperative, they are better able to "identify their own problems, develop their own solutions, and create their own process for successful problem resolution" (Comer et al., 1996). This coaching and leadership through the role of the SDP district facilitator is one that is inherently empowering to the school teams.

The SDP staff actively supports schools in crafting positive *behavior interventions* for students and helping adults develop an understanding that problem behaviors exhibited by children are a result of unmet needs and often can be traced to traumatic home experiences rather than being a product of willful misbehavior. The following example illustrates the SDP approach to helping teachers understand student behavior from a developmental perspective:

> We had a youngster who was 8 years of age, and one Friday he was in rural North Carolina in one of those small, tight communities. His aunt wanted him to get a better education up north. So she drove him up over the weekend and Monday morning, on her way to work, she took the child to school. He was taken directly into the classroom. Now the teacher had three transfers the week before and the last thing she wanted was another child, and she conveyed that without saying a word. The child looked at the teacher and at the strange classroom and he was frightened. And, in panic, he kicked the teacher in the leg and ran out.
>
> That seemed to me like a fairly healthy response, but it's the kind of response that gets a child sent to the principal and punished. Then, when he returns to the classroom, somebody laughs at him, he pops them in the mouth, and then is sent back to the principal. Around and around and around it goes until he is labeled "disturbed."
>
> In this case we had a meeting to talk about what it's like to be eight and have your entire world turned upside down. And the staff understood and came up with ways to help that child in the classroom and help the teacher understand the importance of welcoming and supporting the children. As a result of such experiences teachers responded in a supportive way to children. A bond between children and staff was taking place. Teachers came to realize that the

only difference between their children and the children of middle-income families is that the latter received at home what was necessary to succeed at school. Out of that realization came a program we called Social Skills Curriculum for Inner City Children which is an essential feature of all the schools we work with today. (Comer, 1992, p. 28)

This insight into the causes of behavior altered staff perceptions of students, which in turn altered how staff managed issues that arose. Ultimately, more responsive approaches led to reduced behavior problems and improved relationships. As the teachers and administrators saw benefits, staff would become more willing to apply the principles into each aspect of the school.

Developing parental involvement

Finally, parental involvement must go beyond surface participation as parents are supported to develop their own capacities as partners in educating young people and feel that their voices are welcomed and their ideas are heard. In the early years of SDP implementation, New Haven and Yale staff observed the different ways that parents seemed naturally to choose to participate in schools, and from this, the SDP identified three levels of parent participation. Level 1 is general participation, with parents coming to special events like a holiday concert or an open house. Level 2 participation is more regular and suggests the parents feel they are part of the school community; participation at this level includes parent presence at day-to-day activities by, for example, volunteering in classrooms or helping to organize events and activities. Level 3 participation includes parents who participate on the School Planning and Management Team and take an active role in creating and supporting the vision of the Comprehensive School Plan and bringing other parents along as active members of the school community (Comer & Haynes, 1991). A goal of the program is to get more parents participating at some level, and then to increase the numbers participating more intensively by making the school as welcoming and as accessible as possible—thus ensuring that parents know their voices are heard.

Relational trust among teachers, parents, and school leaders is a key resource that predicts the likelihood of gains in achievement and other student outcomes, provided that instructional expertise is also present. Trust derives from an understanding of one another's efforts and goals, along with a sense of obligation toward each other, grounded in a common mission. As Bryk and Schneider (2002) put it, relational trust is the "connective tissue" that holds improving schools together (p. 144). Relational trust is fostered in stable school communities by skillful school leaders, who actively listen to concerns of all parties and avoid arbitrary actions, and who nurture authentic parent engagement, grounded in partnerships with families, to promote student growth. Positive, trustful relationships among students and teachers can not only facilitate student learning and lead to increased outcomes but also buffer the student from the negative effects of stress, trauma, and adversity (Osher et al., 2018).

In the SDP, parents are an integral part of the school change process, with both the school and the parents being "jointly accountable for children's actions"—something Comer calls the "school-family alliance" (Comer, 1992–93). Unlike more traditional conceptions of accountability, which often just add a few parents to committees to sign off on school improvement plans, the SDP emphasizes the need to welcome and engage parents as partners in an effort to better align students' home life and school life. In this way, parents are assets who, like the staff in schools, can be taught and developed to provide their children with supports to boost the learning happening in the schools. Part of transforming underperforming schools serving low-income and vulnerable populations requires the schools to consider how to support parents in carrying out their responsibilities outside the school and within the family context. As Comer has found, "Educators must work with such parents to extend the school's influence beyond its walls through special trainings and support programs ... and ready access to school professionals for reinforcement" (1992–93, p. 120).

Evidence of Outcomes

When faithfully and fully implemented, the SDP model has been found to produce strong academic, social, and emotional benefits for students. More than three decades of research have demonstrated that schools that have implemented the Comer Process with seriousness over a period of time experience gains in student achievement and evidence of healthy student development, as well as improvements in school culture and functioning.

In 2003, a meta-analysis of 29 comprehensive school reform programs identified the School Development Program as one of only three models that met criteria for the strongest evidence of effectiveness in reliably increasing academic achievement (Borman, Hewes, Overman, & Brown, 2003). The studies examined were from cities across the United States. Research on Comer schools has revealed significant gains in student achievement, behavior, and overall adjustment compared to students in matched control schools (Borman et al., 2003; Haynes & Comer, 1990; Haynes, Comer, & Hamilton-Lee, 1989). Some studies also showed improvements in school climate, as reflected in declines in suspension rates, absenteeism, and corporal punishment (Haynes et al., 1989). A more recent review of well-designed studies found strong improvements in attendance, achievement, and behavior for low-income and/or socially marginalized students in SDP schools (Maier, Daniel, Oakes, & Lam, 2017).

A review of findings from project reports of SDP implementation in San Francisco, California; Chicago, Illinois; Cambridge, Massachusetts; and Washington, D.C., along with published research articles from Chicago and from Prince George's County in Maryland, suggested that these results are achieved as the SDP improves school organization, which facilitates collaboration among staff and increases parent involvement. This improvement contributes to a sense of empowerment and ownership among staff through a shared purpose. The SDP provides a structure and a process to support and bring about systematic changes, as schools show an increased focus on the well-being of students, with child development at the center of education. Schools that incorporate the entire program into the functioning of the school show better results in school attendance and student achievement, and they exhibit a better school climate overall—compared to those that implement only a few features (Haynes, Emmons, & Woodruff, 1998).

To extend the program's reach, the Comer School Development Program combined forces with Edward Zigler's School of the 21st Century at Yale in 1990 to create an even more far-reaching community schools model with wraparound services (Desimone, Finn-Stevenson, & Henrich, 2000). These complementary approaches share the same theoretical base. The Comer-Zigler (CoZi) model integrates services at the school site, transforming the school into a year-round, multiservice center providing services from early morning to early evening. The 21st Century components include year-round, all-day child care that is high quality and developmentally appropriate for children ages 3 to 5; before- and after-school and vacation care for school-age children; outreach and guidance for parents of children ages birth to 3 (e.g., support groups and health and developmental screenings); support and training for family day-care providers in the school neighborhood; and information and referral services for all members of the school community.

The CoZi model was initially piloted in 1990 at an elementary school serving a low-income African American community in Virginia (Desimone et al., 2000) and subsequently over a three-year period at another elementary school in Norfolk beginning in 1992 (Finn-Stevenson & Stern, 1997). Following the success of these initial pilots, the program was evaluated over a three-year period from 1996 to 1999 in Norfolk, Virginia. Results indicated that children achieved higher academic outcomes than a matched comparison group. Strong support from parents and school personnel was also documented (see Dryfoos, 2000).

Over the years, a number of studies have shed light on the kind of implementation that allows strong results to emerge and on the elements of the work that appear to make a difference. For example, a quasi-experimental study of 19 inner-city Chicago schools serving 5th through 8th grade students found the 10 schools that implemented the Comer Process showed a significant gain in reading and mathematics achievement relative to matched control schools. Students in the Comer program reported less acting out (especially in terms of delinquency and mischief outside school), and both students and teachers reported improved academic climates in their schools relative to control schools (Cook, Murphy, & Hunt, 2000).

These results were attained over time as the schools functioned as continuously improving learning communities in which the social and academic dimensions of school climate reinforced each other with a collective emphasis on learning. The initial year of implementation focused on increasing parent involvement, followed the next year by improving social relationships (between principals and teachers, as well as among teachers and between parents and teachers). The last two years involved systemic program efforts to influence classroom change, including modifying curriculum design and coordination, conducting more and better teacher training, and supporting instructional practice through the work of master teachers and principals. These efforts increased the correspondence between the Comer program's support work—which was focusing increasingly on instruction—and Chicago's citywide reform initiative.

Furthermore, longer use of the program and higher-quality implementation were linked to better results (Cook et al., 2000).

Strong implementation occurred in situations where the following had occurred:

- Schools had developed more effective school teams and a more thoughtful school improvement plan.
- All parties had a greater say in governance and could see their feelings and interests taken into account.
- The needs of various cultural and racial groups were taken into account.
- Team members were committed to improving the school.
- Knowledge of child development was used to develop programs and problem-solving strategies.
- Consensus was used throughout the school.

Similarly, a longitudinal case study of 13 schools in a culturally and linguistically diverse urban district found that the two schools implementing the Comer Process sustained a high level of implementation across the four years of the study and yielded better outcomes in math and reading achievement for students relative to their counterparts at matched comparison schools (Datnow, Borman, Stringfield, Overman, & Castellano, 2003).

A randomized controlled study of the Comer School Development Program, conducted in 23 Maryland middle schools (7th and 8th grades) in Prince George's County, highlights the importance of considering the quality of program implementation (Cook et al., 1999). Researchers noted that the program was generally not well implemented in this county, and comparisons showed no overall differences on key outcomes between schools assigned to implement the Comer Model and control schools. However, when the quality of implementation was taken into account, differences emerged. Using a measure that assessed staff perceptions about program implementation and about their functioning in collaborative teams that are part of the Comer Model, students in schools that had higher-quality implementation experienced more positive changes in psychological well-being and commitment to conventional values (upholding the same standard of behavior in and outside school) and showed less increase in absenteeism and less involvement in petty misbehaviors.

Results from research led the Comer team to move to a districtwide dissemination process (Comer & Emmons, 2006). The team observed that when new principals or district leadership did not support the SDP, or a number of teachers who were not trained to use the model joined the staff at the same time, gains that had been hard earned over three to five years could be lost in a few months. A districtwide approach is necessary to promote deep and wide understanding, approval, continuous training, and support for a whole child approach to education. This requires commitment to the process from the district central office, the school board, and the school staff.

In the SDP's work with five districts in the late 1990s, the formal beginning of a systemwide process was marked by the school board designating the SDP as the program to be integrated into district initiatives, with a minimum commitment of five years from the board to support implementation through approval of funds and enacting policies in alignment with the SDP. Where this district approach was adopted, all of the schools in the district were then able to use the SDP framework with the authority and force of the school board and central office behind them. Coherence and continuity across schools was provided by the District Steering Committee, with participation of school teams and representatives from the board and central office.

Overall, the accumulated data support a theory of action in which a positive social climate brings about improvements in academic climate, followed by positive changes in a range of student outcomes. As described in Chapter 3, with leadership and commitment at both the school and district levels, SDP teams can help create a positive school climate that supports and nurtures whole student development. Applying the six developmental pathways to well-planned and focused activities results in and supports positive student outcomes.

3

The School Development
Program in Action
in New Jersey

~~~~~~~~~~~~~~~~~~~~~~~~~~

The School Development Program is not a quick-fix approach to school reform but a means to organize all the structures, processes, and practices of a school around the healthy development of children. It provides knowledge, skills, and strategies to all of the adults in a child's life to allow them to work together toward these ends, and its goals ultimately require all the parts of an education system to engage in a well-orchestrated effort to provide the resources needed to support child development, adult development, and school development.

To illustrate how this work occurs, we tell the stories of how it unfolded in two different settings: in Norman S. Weir School in Paterson, New Jersey, as part of a school finance reform remedy; and, as described in the next chapter, in the New Haven Public Schools in Connecticut, where the program has existed in some form or another for 50 years, since its inception. Each locale has a unique approach to implementing the SDP's nine-part model based on context-specific needs, illustrating that, far from being a prescriptive program, the SDP shifts the mindsets of a school community in service of developing and teaching children in personalized, caring, and cohesive ways.

The State Context

After 30 years of litigation and nine court decisions, equalized funding was finally brought to high-poverty districts in New Jersey through the *Abbott v. Burke* decision, which was ultimately implemented in 1998. This remedy created an influx of $246 million in state "parity" aid to bring per-pupil spending in the 28 (later 30) *Abbott* districts up to the level in the state's 110 successful, suburban districts. Districts could also apply for an additional $312 million in supplemental assistance, which could be spent on curriculum implementation linked to the state standards, whole school reforms, early childhood education or full-day kindergarten, class-size reduction, technology or facilities investments, or health, social services, and summer school programs to help students catch up.

By the time the new resources arrived, however, many of the underresourced, low-wealth districts were so overwhelmed with staff shortages, deferred maintenance, and dysfunctional systems that it took significant work to build functioning systems again (Darling-Hammond, 2010).

The solutions were also affected by the court's initial insistence that each school in the targeted districts had to choose one of the New American Schools' whole school reform (WSR) models. This requirement created incoherence in some school districts, such as Newark, whose 75 schools adopted 10 different models, producing no cohesive approach within or across the schools (MacInnes, 2009). The districts that showed strong progress—Union City, West New York, Perth Amboy, and later Paterson—adopted the Comer Model districtwide, which created a strong student-focused culture in the schools, targeting healthy development and adult collaboration, and then worked from the district level to improve instruction. In the rest of this chapter, we describe how the School Development Program transformed one of the lowest-achieving schools in Paterson.

Norman S. Weir Elementary School[1]

Norman S. Weir Elementary School in Paterson, New Jersey, like hundreds of troubled schools across the United States, had adopted an all too common path to try to boost academic achievement: the school had removed arts and sports programs and doubled up on reading and math instruction as a way to get better scores. This strategy backfired. Scores fell even further, and the school was desperate to find a new model that would work. On the heels of the state's takeover of the district for low performance, Paterson Public Schools had a steep hill to climb to turn around its most struggling schools.

Weir, like other schools in the district, was tasked with identifying a school reform model that would guide its transformation. In 1992, Weir identified the Comer SDP and began the process of implementation. The process of change for Weir was slow and fraught with a number of growing pains. By one account, during the early years, "there was no cohesion within Weir. Each person went in the direction indicated by his or her preferences. There was no common mission or sense of direction" (Emmons, Efimba, & Hagopian, 1998, p. 42). This disarray was compounded by a school climate that was "characterized by student disaffection with the learning process, frequent fights, and low staff morale in a building that was in disrepair" (p. 39).

In the 15 years or so that Norman S. Weir implemented the Comer SDP, it served a very diverse student population that came from all over the city with a first-come, first-served policy. About half of its approximately 300 students identified as African American; about 45 percent as Latino; and roughly 5 percent as white, Asian, or other. Because the school was an inclusion setting for special education, between 30 and 45 percent of students were classified as having disabilities, depending on the year. In addition, 80 to 90 percent

---

[1] This section draws in part from Emmons, Efimba, & Hagopian (1998).

qualified for free and reduced lunch (Emmons et al., 1998; Emmons & Baskerville, 2005).

In 1997, there was a change in leadership in Paterson Public Schools, with a new superintendent who wanted to shake things up in the district office. Ruth Baskerville, the district's director of curriculum and instruction, was reassigned as the principal of Norman S. Weir. Completely unfamiliar with the Comer SDP, Baskerville arrived at Weir ready to learn and support the school during its turnaround process. During her tenure, Norman S. Weir thrived, becoming one of the highest-achieving schools in the district—bright, clean, well maintained, with a staff that was enthusiastic, collaborative, and productively engaging families and community in the school.

Building relationships among staff

As noted earlier, a key aspect of the School Development Program is to support adult development so that the adults can support children's development. Building a positive, collaborative school culture, focused on the development of children, required the Weir faculty and staff to truly engage, with a willingness to be vulnerable and open with one another in genuine partnership. In the same way that children need to feel part of a warm and loving community, so did the teachers need to feel this kind of support. Alongside SDP district facilitator Shelley Leppert, Baskerville described how the establishment of trustful, collaborative relationships among the staff served as the bedrock for transformation at the school. She reflected on the synergy among her staff as a critical component of how and why they were successful in turning around Norman S. Weir:

> I can tell you, teacher retention is a big deal; especially when you're in a troubled district, lots of people leave. They don't want to be there; they don't have to be there; they'll look for other jobs. We had a stable staff, and I credit that to the culture of the Comer school, because the culture

was inviting, so that even with trouble all around, if I'm in a comfortable environment, I'm staying. You know, we really made magic . . . we wrapped around each other. . . . We were just very caring.

This collegial warmth translated to how faculty worked together as well. Using the SDP principles of collaboration, consensus, and no-fault problem solving to guide everything they did as a staff helped to "build trust and a safe environment," according to Leppert.

Building relationships between children and teachers

Research has found positive outcomes for student achievement when schools create more personalized environments providing opportunities for stronger relationships among adults and students. For example, small schools or small learning communities with per-sonalizing structures—such as advisory systems, teaching teams that share students, or looping with the same teachers over multiple years—have been found to improve student achievement, attach-ment, attendance, attitudes toward school, behavior, motivation, and graduation rates (Bloom & Unterman, 2014; Felner, Seitsinger, Brand, Burns, & Bolton, 2007; Friedlaender, Burns, Lewis-Charp, Cook-Harvey, & Darling-Hammond, 2014; Lee, Bryk, & Smith, 1993).

Weir instituted several practices, including looping, to build strong teacher-student relationships. Students looped with teach-ers for two to three years in the elementary school; and in the middle school, students would stay with the same English or math teacher for multiple years as well. Baskerville recalls parents appreciating this practice because they would become more "comfortable" with the teachers and "know their style, their expectations." Shelley Lep-pert echoed this sentiment, saying that looping was instrumental, "allow[ing] the teachers to pick up right where they had left off in June, so there was no down time. Not only did [teachers] know their students very well, they knew what they had already taught them and could build upon. So that really helped to move forward academically with the students."

Strengthening practice

Unlike other reform models that push a certain instructional approach or have rigid guidelines on pedagogy or pacing, the Comer Model instead pushes educators to be the experts; their professional knowledge and expertise is honored, and they are expected to create the sorts of learning experiences that will meaningfully engage students because they, in fact, know the students better than anyone. Leppert lauded this aspect of the Comer Process because in professionalizing the teachers, respecting their knowledge, and empowering them to make curricular and instructional decisions, their sense of efficacy and morale soared; the children benefitted from having teachers who were happy and as engaged in their own work as the students were:

> Some models can be very rigid: you follow this timeline, you follow this script. Comer didn't provide any of that. The teachers instead created it. And they knew their students best so that they could [decide when to] put the children into teams or groups to work on a project; [they knew] to create the group in a way that [students] could work well together, so that they all could share their own strengths, thereby building respect as well as collaboration.

Using the four staff development days allotted per year and the 100 hours of continuing education the state of New Jersey required of its teachers every five years, Baskerville and Leppert created their own version of an in-house Comer conference for staff. During these development days, the various teams would suggest topics to discuss based on needs that had arisen during team meetings around goals and data. This time was used both for educative purposes as well as for team building among the staff. Maintaining positive working relationships and allowing time for people to get to know one another better was an important part of becoming a healthy school community. Once funds ran out for their own professional development, the leadership team rotated which staff would be sent to the Comer Conference in Atlantic City each year, with hopes that over time, everyone would experience the training firsthand. Leppert underscored how attending conferences with SDP faculty and staff from across the country would reignite the staff's enthusiasm:

> There would be an affirmation of what we'd been talking about at home using the developmental pathways as a guide to our lesson planning and our atmosphere in the classroom. Using consensus, no-fault, and collaboration...
> I just think it rejuvenated the staff, and so they came back and were able to buy in, yet again, with more enthusiasm. And it's like anything else—you treat a faculty well and they feel good. The morale was good, the morale was high.

The sense of professional efficacy and pride that came about as a result of the school's efforts at implementing the program proved to be remarkably fulfilling for the students, community, and staff alike.

Creating a school community

To work effectively in schools, the SDP had to overcome suspicions from the community, as they were viewed as outsiders affiliated with an elite university (Comer, 1988). The trust-building needed to address this perception was like that needed to build trust within the schools. Doing so requires principal leadership that is distributed and collaborative. The SDP team worked strategically to help principals see that power sharing through a shared governance structure is one way to increase their ability to manage the school. Shelley Leppert reflected on leadership demonstrated by her principal:

Under the principalship of Dr. Baskerville there was trust built, it was a safe environment. . . . We carried collaboration, consensus, and no fault through everything we did. And I don't think that would have been possible had we not had the administration we had. She wasn't threatened by it; in fact, she cherished it. She looked at it as helpful and inspiring. [She] didn't feel she had to be in charge; her vision of herself was as the educational leader, but not necessarily the boss.

Transforming the school into a community required the leadership at Weir to embrace how the Comer Process underscores the importance of all members of the school community working together in a focused and authentic way—from paraprofessionals and cafeteria staff to parents and principals; no one was incidental or peripheral. As the school culture began to shift, there was nowhere to go but up. As Leppert explained,

I know, personally and professionally, relationships are what makes people go to the end of the earth for you. It's all about that. Well, parents are the same. . . . Once they had some buy-in, once they were valued, then parents started coming. But for the most part, I believe that is the reason that within two years from my coming there, we were at the top of the district, and we had a line wrapped around the school when it came to registration.

Involving parents

Getting to a point where parents recognized the school's achievements and successes, and then translating that enthusiasm to increased registration, did not occur by happenstance. Baskerville recalls how she and her staff went about bringing families into the school and building that sense of community:

[O]ur parents were very skeptical of coming to the school, and they thought things were only going to be punitive. But one of the things that we instituted instantly was [contacting] parents to say, "Your child did super today." So every parent call, in other words, was not "I'm suspending Joey" . . . so that every time the phone rang, [parents would say] "What did my kid do?" which points out their [own] failure; it wasn't that at all. So parents got used to receiving phone calls . . . and it changed the composition of the parent community in the school. . . . That was really good. We had almost no parent involvement, and then, what happened maybe accidentally or maybe it was part of Comer's design, was we discovered the talents parents had . . . I mean, we found all this raw talent. Who knew?

Shelley Leppert explained how creating a "warm, friendly, and family-based" culture encouraged parents to buy in to the SDP process of transformation that was underway:

We did a lot of activities where parents were invited and we fed them and had fun with them. The faculty came out to home-school meetings, which wasn't really that strong of a thing in Paterson, because as you know, Paterson can be difficult, particularly in the evening. But we came out, and that made the relationships stronger as well. We would have family events where the parents came and participated with the students, [like] a pajama reading evening for the lower grades, [or a] family fun night. We tried to bring the families out together, not just for a school meeting, but to have fun together in the school. We also did workshops for parents on Saturdays on relevant topics, [such as] how to help your student with homework, what can you do to encourage more reading, things of that nature.

Once parents were in the building and felt more comfortable hearing from and reaching out to the school, then Baskerville knew they would need to find ways to train the parents on the features of the Comer Method and teach them to understand how important they were to the development of children in the home. As she explained,

> The thing about the training was once you validated parents' worth, they were open to training. So I know in my heart, just being a seasoned administrator, that had we simply put out a flyer or a phone call, a robo call ... and said, "Parents, we're doing Comer," we wouldn't have had anybody; because it would be, like, "Well, what is that? And, how [does] that pertain to me?" ... See, everything is about, one of the best things at Comer, is relationships. . . . Once they had some buy-in, once they were valued, then parents started coming.

Building a school-family alliance is a critical feature of the Comer Process that extends beyond just having a select group of parents participate on the Parent Team or on the School Planning and Management Team. Empowering parents to better support their children, to seek guidance from their peers and the school staff when in need of support, points to a shift in how the family and the school operate in concert with one another. Instead of traditional conceptions that consider schools and families as separate institutions, in the SDP Process, the home and family collaborate to become the "village" that raises the children. Baskerville recalled how she and her team decided to take advantage of the window of time at the beginning of the school year when parents come to campus to pick up schedules and meet their child's new teachers:

> We usually got a good turnout, so of course we took advantage of that. We had refreshments—if you feed them, they will come—and we had little breakout groups so that the

way we structured the very first evening with parents was not just go to the classroom, sit for 20 minutes, meet the teacher, pick up literature, and go home. No . . . we infused Comer . . . we had a video we prepared; we [shared about] the developmental pathways; we had literature, like posters, around; so parents could be exposed a little bit, subtly, and then also directly. We made sure that the teachers had the same message, so that when they were talking about expectations for the year, which parents were interested in, at that very beginning meeting, that's when they were able to sort of infuse the Comer idea. So parents had an expectation that we were dealing with the whole child and not just the academic. . . . Because we learned, probably from school lunch programs, [that] if kids are hungry, they're not ready to learn. So, no, it shouldn't be the school's responsibility to feed the child, but hey, if this is the world we're living in, feed the child. And the same thing with feeding the brain, feed the ego, help them understand who they are and give them ways to explore. And they did.

These sorts of activities, in addition to the more formal participation structures available through the Parent Team and the School Planning and Management Team, help to create an environment that makes the parents as much a part of the school community as the students. Comer (1992–93) articulated the power of such family interactions:

When children observe their parents or other children's parents in schools enjoying the experience and immersed in the life of the school, children identify with the enthusiasm and dedication of these parents and seek to imitate their involvement by immersing themselves in their work and the learning process. They internalize the value of learning as an enjoyable and self-enhancing experience.

> The drudgery of academic involvement is lifted because the home/school dichotomy fades, and school is seen as a continuum. (p. 119)

Developing school outcomes

Perhaps the most compelling part of the Comer SDP is when the academic outcomes match the effort put into creating a positive school climate built on trustful and genuine relationships. Within the first five to six years of the SDP at Weir, test scores began to improve. Shelley Leppert attributes this increase in academic learning to a sense of safety generated by positive relationships schoolwide:

> The children were safe in the classroom environment, just as the teachers were safe with the administration and with each other. And we went from a failing school to a school that was a model of excellence. . . . I think it's because we did study the data, and we would revise our teaching strategies accordingly.

This sense of social, emotional, psychological, and physical safety, combined with active and intentional analysis of student outcomes, was a recipe for success. Because of this sense of safety and trust, the faculty at Weir were able to take feedback from one another, learn from data, and collaborate to find ways to continuously improve. Based on these data, they were also able to modify, adapt, and adopt instructional strategies and schoolwide practices and systems that would not only reinforce the positive relationships that were blooming but also ensure that all members of the team were meaningfully engaged in the maintenance of school growth. From the writing of the Comprehensive School Plan to weekly grade-level cluster meetings, the faculty were part of the planning, and any iterations of the plan were based on real-time information. Shelley Leppert reflected on the power of the weekly meetings where staff could collaborate and problem-solve together:

Those weekly cluster meetings helped the children academically as well because everyone then at the meetings had a finger on the pulse of how the students were doing. If students were having difficulty with another subject area or another faculty member, perhaps another member of the team could give insight. So there really was that family feeling that was built, like the famous quote of James Comer, "it takes a village." In fact, it did, and we were a village.

Baskerville also emphasized the importance of using data to assess and modify curriculum and instruction. Instead of using test results as a means to identify instructional failure, the school used data to inform next steps. As she explained,

We analyzed [data] so that we could stay on top, because I always had an eye towards improvement. We didn't just accept, nor did we allow test scores to go down. There was always a remedy, whether it was a change in the grade level of a teacher, whether it was a change in the makeup of the kids, whether looping helped, because sometimes that was the answer, but we were always in search of the answer. . . . It is so important that you objectively look at data. So yes, we need to look at the school, and that might point out that [in] 4th grade there's a dip in science, or math, or reading, or writing, or whatever. We don't take it personally, and the rest of the grades don't all stand with a finger that points at the 4th grade. So people got comfortable just aggregating data, and even across a grade level, they got comfortable, because we knew it wasn't in a punishing way. And I can't stress that enough—that that is just such an important thing. We just simply said, "Where are we?" and we owned the problem, the whole school, [asking] "So what do we do about that dip in 4th grade?" And then my job . . . was "How can I help? How can I support?"

This frame of reference paid off. In a follow-up study on the progress made at Weir, "Maintaining Excellence While Managing Transitions: Norman S. Weir Revisited" (Emmons & Baskerville, 2005), the authors found the following outcomes attributable to schoolwide improvements associated with the SDP Process:

- In the 2002–03 school year,
  - 95.9 percent of Weir 4th graders achieved full or advanced proficiency on the state language arts literacy test, compared to 52.4 percent of 4th graders in the Paterson District and 77.6 percent of 4th graders statewide.
  - 95.9 percent of Weir 4th graders achieved full or advanced proficiency on the mathematics exam, compared to 43.2 percent of Paterson District 4th graders and 68 percent of New Jersey 4th graders.
- In the 2003–04 school year, 100 percent of Weir 4th graders achieved full or advanced proficiency on both math and language arts exams.
- In a school questionnaire administered by the authors, school faculty and staff reported the school climate as "relaxed," "very good," "terrific." Others described the collegiality among staff as "excellent," with "fantastic" relationships, where "every student and parent is valued."

Baskerville reflected on her tenure at Norman S. Weir as "the most joyous time," while Leppert, similarly nostalgic, called her time there an "educational Camelot."

Although the Comer Program is no longer formally supporting the Paterson schools, the gains made during that era have put the district and individual schools on a stronger footing. Weir Elementary students now achieve as well as the New Jersey state average, even though the school serves many more students in poverty and has much higher rates of students with disabilities. Weir students also continue to grow in their learning at a faster rate than those in other schools (see www.greatschools.org/new-jersey/paterson/1567-Norman-S.-Weir-Elementary-School). As a district, Paterson has achieved a strong turnaround story in which the SDP and developmentally oriented practice played an important role. Paterson now has one of the highest urban graduation rates in the United States at 88 percent—far above the national average for all schools and close to the New Jersey average, which is top-rated in the nation (State of New Jersey Department of Education, www.state.nj.us/education/data/grate/2017).

4

The School Development
Program in Action
in New Haven

~~~~~~~~~~~~~~~~

New Haven, Connecticut, is the birthplace of the SDP Model, and so it is fitting that the local school district, New Haven Public Schools, is a long-standing partner of the program. As former Superintendent of Schools Garth Harries put it, "Dr. Comer and his School Development Program are in the DNA of our school reform efforts in New Haven" (Shelton, 2014).

Although the SDP is an integral part of the educational landscape, implementation of the model in New Haven's schools has been defined by "ebb and flow," explained Fay Brown, director of child and adolescent development at the School Development Program. Over time, "every school had elements, but not every school did Comer in depth." The extent and nature of the SDP's involvement in the city's schools have evolved over time, spurred by developments both within and outside the district. All the same, the model has consistently played an important role in transforming the experiences of learners in schools where it's taken root.

Creating a Developmental Approach to School Reform

The Comer Model took root in the late 1960s, at the height of the civil rights movement, in an era of increasing concern about the futures of children in the United States who were being excluded from the nation's economic and social opportunities (Comer et al., 1996). It was also a time when the "Ford Foundation and other foundations were urging universities to use their resources to help address this issue," explained Comer. For those working at the Child Study Center, the schools were an obvious place to pursue the important work of promoting the well-being of young children. Comer observed,

> It occurred to me that the only place where you could support development, when it wasn't supported well at home, was in the schools. The real motivation was when I realized that there's nothing for the child who does not receive support at home or in a network, where there are relationships that are meaningful. . . . If they don't receive that kind of interaction, there is only one other place you could see it and that's in schools—public schools. But the public schools I ran into were terrible, so I knew there was a need to change schools and eventually have schools impact families and communities so that they change the way they prepare children for school.

With this developmental philosophy as motivation, Comer and his colleagues began working in partnership with two New Haven elementary schools, Martin Luther King Jr. and Susan E. Baldwin, to strengthen the learning experiences afforded to students there. Both were among the district's lowest-performing schools academically, and both experienced significant behavioral challenges.

Rebuilding community in schools

To start the work, a team that included Comer, a social worker, a psychologist, and a special education teacher sought to "immerse [them]selves in the schools to learn how they function[ed]" (Comer, 1988, p. 43). This approach was important not only for gathering information to inform the design of the model but also for establishing trust with the school community. New Haven parents were wary of the idea of Yale researchers coming into schools to conduct research—so much so that a group of parents even marched on one of the schools in the first year of the partnership. As a result, there was an agreement from the start that the Child Study Center "wouldn't focus on imposing an intervention on people," explained Comer. To Comer, this represents a "critical difference" between the SDP model and other school interventions:

> We went in with the approach that we would live in the schools, learn about how they worked and what it was they were trying to accomplish. Not tell them how to do it, but to provide our expertise in helping them accomplish what they want to accomplish. And that's how our work is different. . . . We said it's not our intervention, it's their intervention. It's what they do for their kids. And eventually we realized that it has to be what the kid wants for himself or herself.

This deep engagement in the daily happenings of the schools informed the development of the Comer Process. Seeing teachers and administrators in disagreement about the schools' goals, for example, helped the SDP team realize that the project, and the schools themselves, would benefit from structures to help school staff coordinate planning and goal setting. Likewise, observing interactions among teachers, staff, and students underscored the high level of distrust between home and school and the importance of positive interactions between parents and school staff.

It was on the basis of these (and other) findings that Comer and his colleagues developed the nine-part School Development Program. Parents were engaged at the school at multiple levels—attending events and school activities and weighing in on governance issues. A group of mental health professionals—including the school psychologist, social worker, and a special education teacher—would gather to address students' behavioral and learning difficulties. The School Planning and Management Team brought representatives of all the adult stakeholders in a school—from principal and teachers to parents and support staff—together to discuss the schools' programs and procedures. When they gathered, the team members strove to make decisions by consensus and focus on problem solving rather than placing blame. And although the principal's authority was acknowledged, school administrators weighed the opinions of others on the team.

From the start, relationships have been at the heart of the model because of the important role that relationships play in creating a positive climate for development and learning. The Comer Process was designed to give the adults in schools the strategies and structures to "work out ways of working together so that [they] met the needs of children," Comer explained. The adults who participated in the SPMT, for example, were tasked with solving problems, but they were also required to do so "while establishing goals and strategies for the entire school that would create a positive school culture that enables the adults to get along with each other so that they were available to support the development of the kids."

The SDP team continued working with King and Baldwin for the next five years. Over that time, both schools saw academic achievement rise to some of the highest levels in the city and behavioral problems noticeably decline (Comer & Emmons, 2006). With the model well instantiated in the school communities, SDP staff turned their attention to expanding the use of the model to other schools in New Haven.

Staff development was a key mechanism for facilitating the expansion. Trainings gathered representatives from districts across the United States, including New Haven, to learn the fundamentals of the Comer Model and facilitate its implementation in their districts. Although the nine parts of the Comer Model remained stable as the model gained traction, schools and districts retained the freedom and flexibility to tailor its use to meet their specific needs.

It was this freedom that first attracted Dietra Wells, who was a teacher at Katherine-Brennan School in New Haven (the third school to pilot the model) before she became Brennan's principal, then New Haven's director of instruction, and later the district SDP facilitator. She noted,

> [What I always liked about the Comer Process was] that you could tailor it to your own needs. You could do your self-assessment of your school and decide what areas you need to really focus on to help build that foundation to support students.

The other selling point for Wells was the power of collaboration that the process engendered. She explained,

> Before the Comer program, I felt myself working to just change my students. When there was more collaboration and more focus on assessment, [I realized] that we really were not a good school unless everybody was successful. It changed the mindset of what we needed to do: If I have something that's working, I should share it with my colleagues, and I [should focus on] the whole school, that we all set examples of what type of environment we want for them to learn in, and what type of relationships we want, not just for ourselves with parents, but for all the teachers and everyone that is involved. That was very impactful for me, because it wasn't something that you could do alone. If you want true success in your work, then you must work together, in [and] out of school, and at the central office as well.

Taking a developmental approach to literacy

To meet schools' needs, the SDP also developed more direct instructional supports.

In the 1990s, for example, the SDP piloted a program, initially at the Davis Street School, to support elementary students facing challenges with literacy. The program, called Essentials of Literacy, combines the child-centered, developmental approach of the Comer Method with evidence-based strategies for enhancing the literacy skills of young readers. It is built on eight "fundamentals of literacy," including vocabulary development, story writing, and guided reading, and also takes into consideration each student's individual developmental trajectory along all six developmental pathways.

By taking this developmental approach, the program moves beyond reading instruction to support learning and development in other areas, such as boosting confidence and self-esteem. As in other facets of the SDP, parents and families are central; parent volunteers help with reading instruction in the schools, and children without access to books receive materials to take home (Brown & Murray, 2005).

The program was well received by teachers and principals, as well as district leaders. Eleanor Osborne, a former associate superintendent in the district, said, "This new reading program, Essentials of Literacy, was providing students the individualized instruction they needed in the core elements of literacy . . . in an environment that also promoted their social and psychological development" (Brown & Murray, 2005, p. 194).

In the years after the pilot, and with the support of Osborne and others, the model was taken up at schools across the district—reaching 23 buildings by 1999–2000. The program was effective for students. District data from those schools indicated that participating students gained a year-and-a-half or two years of improvement in the space of a single school year (Brown & Murray, 2005). The district expanded the program still further in the summer that followed, modeling elements of its mandatory summer school program after the EOL model, reaching nearly 600 students.

Holding on to a whole child approach

Even in New Haven, the Comer SDP model became less of a focus after the introduction of No Child Left Behind in 2001 radically altered the landscape of schooling, said Iline Tracey, a director of instruction for New Haven Public Schools: "Under No Child Left Behind, Comer went out the door because everything was about academics, academics, academics. Nothing about the social-emotional challenges that students have." The era also ushered in "a few years where there were other initiatives that came into the district that seemed to have taken priority over the Comer Model, in terms of their visibility," explained Fay Brown.

During this relative lull, however, some teachers and principals familiar with the approach continued to apply Comer principles in their classrooms and buildings. According to Brown, "If you walked into several of those schools, even during that time, there were administrators who would be saying, 'We are a Comer school.'... There were individual schools that still maintained a strong Comer focus." This continued interest in the SDP model persisted in some corners of the district and, combined with recognition of a widening achievement gap, led to a renewed interest in the model (Garriga, 2005).

The district's then-superintendent, Reginald Mayo, had himself been trained in the Comer Process during his time as a middle school principal in New Haven and valued the model's holistic approach to the needs of students. He recalled how he had promoted a developmental approach during his time as principal:

> I used to tell my people [teachers and staff] that I know I talk to you most of all about the academic piece, but we have to worry about our kids and how they behave. And we want them to behave in a way and in a situation that is going to make us proud of them and them proud of themselves . . . that they're going somewhere. We've got to develop these kids all the way up and down a spectrum. The Comer

spectrum was that the social or physical, the academic, the social-emotional—all that stuff is what we're about, not teaching to one aspect. . . . It takes all of these things for these kids to be successful.

Mayo worked with SDP staff to craft the district's revived approach to the model, which emphasized the faithful replication of all of its components in a select number of schools (Bass, 2009). Fay Brown explained,

It was then, in 2007, that the superintendent called Dr. Comer and me into his office and he said to us, "Fay Brown, Jim Comer, I need to get serious again with doing Comer in the district. What do we need to do to get Comer back into the district?" And so we said to him, "Well, if we're going to do it this time, we've really got to do it well. We want a small number of schools to start with, where we can go deep with a small number of schools."

The district included seven schools in the renewed effort, eventually expanding it to include 10 schools that received training and supports for implementing the SDP approach.

To turn the model into on-the-ground reality, the district not only contracted with the SDP to provide training and support for school staff but also hired a district SDP facilitator. That position gave a district employee dedicated time to focus specifically on working with schools and staff who were engaged in implementing a developmental approach in their buildings. A long-time district employee with previous training in the SDP model was selected for the position, which enabled her to build strong relationships with the community as well as with SDP staff. This district-SDP collaboration extended to district leadership as well. Superintendent Mayo "always wanted to stay in the know," said Brown, and the district developed a structure that fostered ongoing conversation between the two organizations.

"We used to meet monthly with the superintendent and his folks, a group that he convened for us, to talk about what was going on in these 10 schools."

These district-level structures helped bring support close to the ground, where it could be tailored to the specific needs and goals of school communities rather than following a prescribed set of procedures. School Development Program staff relied on data gathered from surveys of and conversations with students, parents, teachers, and staff, as well as attendance at SPMT or SSST meetings, to determine what types of training and expertise might help schools accomplish their aims. Sheila Brantley, the district SDP facilitator during the mid-2000s revival, underscored the model's responsiveness to the specific needs and strengths of a building:

> [The training] was delivered from the bottom up. What does the school need? What does the principal need? Often we would sit and listen to their concerns and try to problem-solve with them, try to find a way to move the whole staff.

Brantley and the SDP staff would work with the schools to analyze data and identify steps forward. In short, "Whatever a school asked for, we delivered." Brantley described a climate challenge that the team identified in one school based on these data:

> We [said], "In your teacher survey you said that we feel all kids feel accepted and cared for, et cetera, but in your student survey, 80 percent said that they did not feel they could trust the adults. . . . What do we do with the space? How do we balance that? How do we shift that?" And then we help[ed] them come up with strategies and come up with activities so that they could actually see the results and make a difference.

Relationship-building activities were one important strategy used in that school, including exercises that were often as simple as ice-breakers during a morning advisory period. In New Haven, these district investments in key personnel helped to ensure that the Comer Process remained true to its roots as a model designed to respond to the context and climate of specific buildings.

Strengthening practice

Although the specific focus of the supports that the SDP offered to schools varied, staff development was consistently a key part of the process, as Brown explained:

> One of the things that we start off with is to provide professional development because we really do believe that if schools are going to implement the model well, they need to learn what it is, they need to learn the elements.

In educating adults about the fundamentals of the Comer Process—subjects such as the three guiding principles and the developmental pathways—SDP staff used hands-on learning opportunities that engaged teachers as learners. As Cynthia Savo, a lecturer at Yale's Child Study Center who works for the SDP, explained,

> We do a lot of things that require people to actually work together. So instead of just talking about collaboration, we might do a build-the-tower activity where they're given a set of materials and they have to see who could build the highest tower. So there's a certain level of experience where it's not just cognitive. It's just like how we feel about kids and development. It's not just about cognitive.... You need to figure out, "How are we going to work together on this?"

In one professional development session, Savo led a simple activity to promote relationship building among participants. In her words,

"You would partner with somebody and find out: What is their name? How did they get their name? Are they named after somebody? Do they like their name? Do they have nicknames?" Although it appears simple, the activity "really get[s] at kind of deeper issues that relate to the relationships," she explained. "It was a very powerful activity because there were people in the room who basically tell people the wrong name because they thought people would not be able to pronounce their name. And your name is your identity." The activity doubles as a lesson on building relationships that teachers can take back to their classrooms. "[Learning names] is a way to show respect, and it's an initial connection you can have with them. If you're sitting in a classroom and the teacher's been saying your name wrong all year, that doesn't feel too good."

To help teachers apply the strategies that they learned during training, formal professional development was often combined with informal observation and coaching by facilitators with deep knowledge of the SDP model. Fay Brown recalled her time offering these types of supports at one New Haven school:

> I spent a lot of time at Davis Street School just literally sitting in classrooms observing teachers—not from an evaluative perspective . . . but from a Comer relationship perspective. . . . Many of them [teachers] invited me to just observe what they're doing, to see how much they were doing Comer in their classroom, and then to give them some feedback in terms of areas they could improve upon when it comes to the pathways or the guiding principles and so forth.

The district SDP facilitator, Sheila Brantley, could also often be found in classrooms at the Comer schools. In one instance, a teacher requested her support in integrating the developmental pathways into her daily instruction after a training session, so Brantley used modeling to help drive the lesson home:

[The teacher] was teaching a period of history in the twenties. . . . I went in and all the kids were doing research projects. . . . One was working on Al Capone. . . . So we talked about ethical choices. We had the pathways wheel in the front, and I used every single one of [the pathways]. Then I broke them up into small groups. I said, "Turn to your partner and talk about it. So, what kind of language did you use?" So we went through all six pathways, and it showed the teacher that you don't just teach the pathways as a separate thing; you need to integrate it. It becomes the way your classroom operates.

The SDP training and supports led to the application of new approaches to the challenges faced in some of the district's buildings and classrooms. For example, one New Haven teacher, Larissa Giordano, used "pathways journals" as a strategy for improving the climate of her 4th grade classroom after receiving SDP training. The journals were a place where "students could record their learning about each of the pathways and also reflect on their growth along each pathway." The journals also included a "please help me" section "where students were encouraged to write about any issue of concern. They needed to identify the problem, explain it in terms of the pathway to which it was connected, and then propose a solution for solving that problem." The exercise gave Giordano a new means of communicating with her students. She would often respond in writing, though when the situation demanded, she would act more immediately, having one-on-one strategy sessions to address their concerns. For example, when a student wrote about an argument she had with her mother before coming to school, the teacher let her call home to patch things up so she could better focus on her learning. When another wrote with dread about a forthcoming writing exercise, Giordano provided a quick pep talk. The teacher found that the process of journaling and reflection produced benefits for her students:

The plan I implemented in my classroom not only helped to reduce conflicts among students and helped to improve their prosocial behavior, but it also impacted their learning in ways that surprised me as I watched them take risks in their learning. Not only did their confidence increase, but so did mine as I watched my fourth-grade students develop into a community of learners. (Comer, Giordano, & Brown, 2012, p. 456)

Building partnerships with parents

At its heart, the Comer Process is about building, restoring, or maintaining positive relationships in schools for the benefit of children's learning and development. Students' families are important partners in this work, and the Comer Process has changed the ways that school staff interact with students and their families. Consistent with the SDP model, the schools' work on the Comer Process also extended beyond teachers to include students, parents, and other stakeholders. Brantley explained,

We not only worked with just teachers and administrators, but we worked with parents. We did trainings for parents. We support[ed] parents and also students and student leaders and the community. . . . We also included them in our School Planning and Management Teams so that they were part of the voice, part of the opportunity to make changes.

During her time as district SDP facilitator, Brantley also worked with parents to organize a monthly, citywide PTO meeting that used the Comer Process and facilitated learning about consensus, collaboration, and no-fault problem solving.

This inclusive approach is a key part of the Comer Process and was evident in schools such as the Columbus Family Academy. Under the leadership of then-principal Abie Benitez, that school embraced a developmental approach and engaged parents and students as partners in applying the developmental lens to student learning. Benitez explained, "If we were going to do anything, we had to enlist every stakeholder in anything we did." One year, the school zeroed in on the developmental pathways and engaged both parents and staff in learning about them:

> We had a plan for the year that required everybody to focus on a pathway on a weekly basis. And we made sure my announcements were relevant to that pathway. If we had parent meetings that month . . . things had to be connected to the pathways we were learning about. Parent meetings were organized around what pathways we were developing. We would have activities that would support that and that parents could take home and work [on] with kids. A lot of the work we did with parents was to help them become our partners in helping their kids learn.

Benitez and her staff also used morning meetings to immerse their students in understanding their own development and learning. As she described it,

> When we said we were going to talk about pathways, we didn't only speak about pathways with teachers. We talked about it with kids. Kids were trained to understand what the pathways were. They were able to articulate which pathway was impeding them [from] engag[ing] in their learning. They had to think of ways that they could improve their pathway development. So all of that was done through morning meetings and discussions.

Parent engagement was also evident in other district schools, such as Nathan Hale Elementary, which reported particular success in connecting with families through evening workshops (Smith, 2011).

In recent years, there has been increasing attention to parental engagement in addressing students' behavioral and academic needs. As Fay Brown noted,

> [Student and Staff Support Teams] are paying so much attention to student needs and student behaviors, bringing in parents when they're having discussions about that parent's child on the team, getting the parents' input. Some schools who would never [have] thought [to] include parents in those discussions . . . learned how to really bring parents in when they are talking about those parents' children, to hear from the parents their perspective about whether the child is behaving the same way at home, behaving differently. What do they try at home? What can they share with the school? . . . The parents felt it was a partnership.

Benitez concurred, noting that parents have become an active voice in school affairs:

> My parents are the big voices in this city when it comes to saying that it is not a no-fault process when you [district staff] decide what you're going to do and you don't include us. It is not consensus. It is not collaboration. I mean, they're calling it constantly.

As an outgrowth of this work, in recent years, New Haven Public Schools has begun collecting school-climate data from surveys of parents, teachers, and students across all of its schools, not just those implementing the SDP. The surveys cover topics ranging from academic expectations and communication to collaboration and safety. The data for the district as a whole, and for individual schools, have been made available on easy-to-read report cards to support dialogue with parents and community members (New Haven Public Schools, n.d. b).

The SDP is also expanding its work with parents in New Haven. The center recently piloted a peer-to-peer parent education program for parents of young children. That effort trained a small cohort of parents to lead conversation groups with community members focused on child development. Camille Cooper, director of training and learning at the SDP, explained how the Parents, Partners, and Peers initiative that she coordinates offers parents specific training on the developmental pathways as a way of intentionally building parents' capacity to more fully participate in school:

> We talk about the six developmental pathways in depth. We talk about the different aspects of nutrition, sleep, brain development, and how to support the psychological development of their children, the importance of attachment. [The training] really focuses on the different aspects of developing language, of spiritual and ethical development, of physical development . . . ways that parents can support students' cognitive development in their everyday activities . . . how they can really pay attention to how they are psychologically supporting their child, how they are incorporating an understanding of [their children's] emotions and feelings. For example, children watch television, so what are some ways [parents] can help their children think about things a little differently when they're watching television? Asking their children questions about who the character is, where the character is, how do the characters feel? And how to make it a more meaningful experience for them, and to think about what they're watching.

This parent training is similar to a train-the-trainer model: after the five-day intensive training, parents commit to gathering three to six family members, friends, or parents from the school or church to have a conversation about the developmental pathways and reteach the curriculum they just received over a 10-week period. The logic behind this approach is that because the parents are from the community and have similar cultural backgrounds and mutual respect with other parents, the parents they are teaching will feel more receptive and open to this new information and will be more apt to ask questions, voice concerns, and seek help in trying new strategies at home.

This pilot training program culminated with an evening celebration that brought all of the parent trainers and their small networks of parents to the Yale Child Study Center for a mini graduation, replete with a certificate of completion. Cooper explained that this program "really developed community at the two pilot schools, and many of the participants shared that they now have other parents that they can depend on, talk with, and get support from when they are having challenges. One parent actually said, 'I don't scream at my kids anymore. I try to listen to what they have to say and try to understand their behavior.'"

Developing a productive school climate

The goal of the Comer Process is to create a positive school climate in which students can develop and learn effectively. Students are eloquent about how learning about developmental pathways and problem-solving practices helps them contribute to the climate. For example, these 4th and 5th grade students at Davis Street Magnet School commented about morning meeting, which was one of several supports for their social-emotional development (Comer & Savo, 2009):

> You get to interact with other people and tell them what you feel instead of bubbling up and keeping it inside and then it hurts. But you get to let it out and nobody blames you or says "no I didn't" or stuff like that. Instead you get to tell them what's wrong and you get to work it out. —Brianna

I think morning meeting is good because it helps kids with their problems. Like for me, it helps me a lot this year. I used to be getting into a lot of trouble. But then when I learned the Comer pathways, I kind of changed a little. Last year I was getting into trouble and stuff, so now I don't.... [The pathways that have helped me] are the cognitive, the language, and the social. I learned how to think before I act. —Shemar

Morning meeting means a lot to me because it helps me with my day. If I had a problem, like yesterday afternoon, I can bring it up to the class and I can go face-to-face with the person to tell him how I felt about the problem that we had. And it means a lot because it's taught me the ethical pathway, how to talk to people so you don't hurt their feelings when you're asking them to do something or to give them anything. —Rachel

When I see people work out their problems, it really helps me. And I take what they've done and I work out my problems and do the same that they did. —Jahymal

Benitez commented on how efforts to productively engage families and support students' development across a range of domains created tangible differences in the climate of the Columbus Family Academy when she was principal there:

Prior to being in a Comer environment, I saw isolation, I saw silence, I saw lack of self-assurance. So you have these people that at any given moment will spark a conflict because they are not learning to communicate. But when you walk into a Comerized building, you see the bustle of people trying to connect with each other, and we may not agree with things, but we know we are here for the kids, not for us.

She also noted a shift in the reputation of the school in the broader community:

We also were [at] the bottom of the list in New Haven. Many families did not want to attend Columbus. This was not . . . the choice. And by the time I left it was a school [that had], and continues to maintain, a pretty good status in our community and in our city.

This story of success in enhancing school climate was repeated elsewhere in the district, including in a school formerly led by Iline Tracey. When Tracey took the helm, the school was in its first year—the product of merging two existing schools, each with its own culture and way of doing business. In tackling the challenging work of creating a new, unified school culture, Tracey relied on the Comer SDP model:

Merging both cultures was a difficult task. . . . I had to merge both cultures into one, and I think using the Comer development model—especially the School Planning [and] Management Team [and] the Student Staff Support Team—those two systems and structures helped us glue things together.

Tracey described the results of these changes in her building:

[With the IB program], coupled with the Comer school development process, we were able to move the school from failure to success. We came off the state list [of low-performing schools] in two or three years. . . . We rocked and rolled with all these systems. . . . You hear about these systems, but to actually implement them and see them working, it was a powerful experience that I still forever remember because it is riveted in [my] mind how we made the change at the school. . . . After a while, we had long waiting lists. People [were] knocking our doors down to come into King Robinson School, and that to me was powerful. Powerful.

Creating a Whole Child, Whole School, Whole Community Approach

More recently, the emphasis of SDP's efforts in New Haven has shifted away from in-depth implementation of the approach in a cluster of buildings toward supporting a larger number of schools in adopting key pieces of the SDP Model. This change reflects a shift in the needs and interests of the district, brought on in part by changes in the broader policy landscape.

In 2011, the state of Connecticut passed legislation requiring low-performing schools—those identified as being in need of improvement because they failed to achieve adequate yearly progress in test scores—to create school governance councils to engage parents and community members in boosting student achievement. (For more information on the governance councils, see www.cga. ct.gov/current/pub/chap_170.htm#sec_10-223j.) In form and function, these governance councils were in many ways comparable to the Comer Model's School Planning and Management Teams, long required in all New Haven schools, as specified in the local teachers union contract. This similarity was not lost on the district, explained Fay Brown:

> When New Haven received their list, they had many schools—like 20-something schools—on that list of schools that had to have the council. Well, they looked at what the council was mandated to do, the responsibilities of the council, [and] the superintendent and a couple other people in central office said, "Hold on a second. These look just

like the responsibilities of [the] Comer School Planning and Management Team. . . . Why should we disband that and put in place something that is so similar?"

As a result, these nearly two dozen schools, newly focused on strengthening their School Planning and Management Teams, became a priority in the district's Comer efforts.

This shift toward broader engagement with the SDP model across a larger number of district schools was reinforced in 2014, after the district received federal funding from a Teacher Incentive Fund grant to enhance teacher development, evaluation, and compensation. As part of that effort, the district created a position known as "student support facilitator"; these facilitators were tasked with coordinating supports and services for children with social-emotional needs. The role was designed as a teacher leadership opportunity, complete with compensation ($5,000 per year). These facilitators worked within each school's Student and Staff Support Team (or, in cases where no such team existed, the facilitators created one), taking up concerns raised by teachers or staff about specific students, but also "look[ing] at clusters, trends," explained Sheila Brantley, who provided training and supports for the facilitators. "What's coming through your SSST; what are the major complaints?" Every New Haven school had an SPMT, and thanks to the new initiative, nearly all developed an active SSST as well.

Focus on staff development

True to the model, staff development continued to play an important role in implementing the Comer Process as implementation spread across the district, said Fay Brown. "We did broad training districtwide, first of all, but then we went into individual schools, and we did on-site training in literally all of those schools."

District leaders were highly supportive of providing staff with the training they needed to implement a developmental approach. Not only did the district have a contract with the SDP for training, but the district also hired two experienced staff, former district Comer facilitator Sheila Brantley and retired school principal Joe Montagna, to support the adoption of a developmental approach. Both brought a deep understanding of the Comer Process and the context of the district's schools.

As Brantley recounted, "I had just come out of a relationship with many of the schools. I knew their inner workings. I knew which relationships could be even developed more or which were going to be a challenge. So we divided up the schools . . . and then we help[ed] support those facilitators." Brantley even worked with the citywide student council to support them in developing leadership through the lens of the whole child. In Brantley's words, "We had our tentacles all over, with students, with parents, with SSSTs, with the principals."

Trainings and support often focused on understanding child development, the guiding principles, and other cornerstones of the SDP model. For example, Camille Cooper conducted a training that seeks to help teachers learn to address common behaviors in productive, developmentally appropriate ways. In the workshop, teachers are provided a description of about 25 behaviors that may be considered inappropriate—from passing notes and whispering to hitting or name calling. Teachers talk through the behaviors and their responses. "The whole point," Cooper explained, is that "you know children are going to do these things. So let's think, be thoughtful and planful about number one—what can we do to prevent it? And then what would we do to intervene in a developmentally appropriate way?" Cooper provided an example of how this approach might translate into a classroom setting:

> Around [age] 11 or 12, children have become a little more argumentative or they're pushing back. And this is really natural because they are kind of coming into their own and formulating their own ideas and opinions. But rather than trying to keep children from doing that, you incorporate

within your instruction having debates or looking at "compare and contrast" so that they can naturally be against something or for something. Because at that age level they're going to be against things and they're going to push back. So this was a way of incorporating something that is a natural behavior that children would have in a particular age group and understanding it, to utilize it as a part of your instructional strategy.

The activity sought not only to enhance adults' understanding of children but also to leverage that understanding to the benefit of classroom instruction.

Staff development has also included opportunities for school staff to learn from their peers. The SDP had begun convening SPMT and SSST chairpersons to exchange best practices, and when the student support facilitators were introduced, they also had meetings focused on sharing their knowledge, explained Brantley. The facilitators were "taking what they learned from us back into their schools, helping to make a difference in the schools, [both] on the broad level of the schools and in individual classrooms and with individual teachers. And then they're coming back next month and they're sharing challenges or successes with us, with one another."

These meetings were not the only opportunities to share learning across schools. The SDP staff also facilitated the sharing of effective tools and processes through their attendance at individual SPMT and SSST meetings. In some cases, staff even brought people from one school to observe high-functioning teams at another in an effort to strengthen their implementation of the Comer Process.

Although the grant that supported the student support facilitator has ended, the SDP and New Haven Public Schools are continuing to find opportunities to equip district staff with the knowledge and skills to implement a developmental approach in schools. The SDP continues to work with district schools' SPMTs and SSSTs and recently had the opportunity to provide training in the Comer Process to central office staff for the first time, with workshops focused on effective communication and the developmental pathways.

Through New Haven's work on the Comer Process, student learning has been put at the center of school reform, explained Iline Tracey, who has more than 30 years of experience in New Haven. "Through the Comer Process, everything brings to bear on what we need to do for students. It is very much student centered. And we're using the adults to help to push student-centered learning."

This philosophy is reflected in the district's "School Change Initiative," which envisions students at the center of a system that surrounds them with teachers, schools, and wraparound services to support their development academically and personally, and to promote their success in college, career, and life (New Haven Public Schools, n.d. a).

Accomplishing this type of student-centered approach in schools requires productive problem solving by adults on behalf of the students. Sheila Brantley noted,

> I see SSST teams taking global issues and diving deep: taking the lead in wellness campaigns for children and adults, creating crisis funds for students experiencing a sudden funeral or homelessness, and having courageous conversations around school climate. I see teams learning about immigration, providing support and education so the students and their families can seek help and the educators understand the laws and responsibilities. I see teams being proactive, analyzing data trends from referrals, looking at areas of concern, grades, and creating prevention strategies. I see more SSSTs talking about strengths rather than deficits and using positive comments....
>
> I see adults with compassionate hearts, astute minds, growth mindsets, and positive energy to change the [lives] of children looking at me.

Creating developmentally supportive classrooms

Research on classroom management shows that productive classrooms are organized not around a compliance regimen that emphasizes the recognition and punishment of misbehavior, but on the promotion of student responsibility through the development of common norms and routines with the participation of students (LePage, Darling-Hammond, & Akar, 2005). Students may help develop the classroom rules and norms and take on specific tasks—ranging from managing materials to leading activities in the class-room—that allow them to be responsible and contributing members of the community. Developing an intentional community ensures a sense of belonging and safety, with shared norms represented in all of the school's activities. In addition, a culture of participation encour-ages student agency and leadership (Darling-Hammond, Cook-Harvey, Flook, Barron, & Osher, forthcoming).

In line with this knowledge base, SDP schools create classrooms defined by warm and accepting communities of learners. Cynthia Savo, who works for the SDP, describes how developmental knowl-edge was used in one case to help address challenges with the climate in a middle school classroom:

> We were talking about behavior issues in the middle grades, and I asked [the SSST] to think about the developmental tasks of middle schoolers. What do they need? And I said that I thought that one of the things they need is roles and that if we focus on having a healthy classroom community and that people have roles, everybody contributes. . . . The thing is, people think that once kids have big bodies, that somehow they don't like all that stuff, but it's not true at all.

Looking for a way to incorporate this developmental under-standing into the classroom, the group found inspiration in an early childhood classroom, where all students were given a role to play from a list of rotating jobs, complete with laminated badges. The team translated the system for a middle school context, said Savo. "Someone was the concierge. They had five table washers. They had a meteorologist, and somebody went and got the snacks in the morning in the cafeteria." Not only was there "incredible vocabulary," but the project also made an impact in the classroom:

> [The students] loved it. They loved walking around with their badges. It instilled a sense of "we're all working together. This is our classroom. We keep it clean, we share, we take care of people." And it spread outside the classroom because they were proud of having these roles. . . . It's the concept of positive classroom community, having a role, and doing something that's developmentally supportive.

This developmental understanding had implications for approaches to discipline, as well. Sheila Brantley explained,

> Where it used to be very easy to say that this kindergartener or that 1st grader threw a chair [and say,] "Well, suspend him for four days," with the help of the schools understanding child development, we've helped them realize that suspending a kindergartener or a 1st grader is not a solution. The solution is to understand the behavior and what is underneath it and what we can do in the classroom to change the environment to ensure that this child is successful.

Individual schools have begun to use systems such as Positive Behavioral Interventions and Supports or restorative justice to significantly reduce the use of exclusionary discipline (Peak, 2018), and the district is now explicitly moving toward a more developmentally supportive approach that replaces exclusionary strategies like suspension and expulsion with practices that are educative and restorative for students. In line with the work some schools have been doing with SDP, the New Haven 2016–17 district code of conduct notes the following:

> A team of educators, leaders, parents and community partners is working on a plan around restorative practices, which is a strategy that aims to
>
> 1. Foster learning through positive relationships and interactions with peers;
> 2. Help educators recognize the importance of keeping the social and emotional health of their students a deliberate and central focus of learning;
> 3. Ramp up efforts to strengthen safe and supportive schools, address conflict, improve school climate, and build a positive school culture; and
> 4. Recognize the impact of trauma and loss on our youth; and the need to use restorative strategies that includes consequences and accountability for those who have caused harm and restorative justice to repair the harm for those who have suffered from destructive actions. (New Haven Public Schools, n.d. c)

This recognition of the effects of trauma is critically important for the design of needed developmental supports. Adversity happens in all communities, and healthy development does as well. However, poverty and racism, together and separately, create increased risks as they make the experience of chronic stress and adversity more likely (Shonkoff et al., 2012). As discussed in Chapter 1, when adversity is severe, prolonged, or when the counteracting effects of stable relationships are missing, the body adapts to the continual activation of the stress response system by going on "high alert" and staying there. This situation produces excessive levels of cortisol that flood the brain and other vital organs, disrupting their normal functioning. The stress response also helps to explain how unbuffered stress can affect educational outcomes. Traumatic or strongly emotional events can simultaneously interfere with emotion regulation, induce physiological arousal, and impair cognitive function (for a review, see Cantor et al., 2018).

Schools, families, and communities can buffer the effects of stress, as some SDP schools in New Haven have done. As Cynthia Savo explained,

> There are certain things that happen over the course of the school year. They're totally predictable. We know how things are going to be before and after a holiday break or winter break. We know that there are times of the year that really trigger kids: the holidays, Mother's Day, Father's Day. There are things that kids experience, especially kids who have experienced trauma, that are going to be hard for them. So some schools have been proactive. They've actually mapped out the stress levels. What are the stress levels for the kids? What's October like? What's March like? What is that like for the staff? For the parents?

By understanding when stress is likely to arise, schools can work to create strategies and systems "to address it without instruction necessarily having to come to a grinding halt."

Preparing Teachers for Developmentally Grounded Education

For developmentally grounded education to become routine and to be sustained, it is essential to transform the preparation of educators. Alongside efforts to redesign district and school practices, the SDP has launched an initiative with a local teacher preparation program to create a pipeline of teachers who are prepared for these practices.

Southern Connecticut State University (SCSU), home to Connecticut's largest teacher preparation program, is trying to strengthen the state's developmentally prepared teacher pipeline through a collaboration between the university, four SDP schools in New Haven School District, and Yale's Center for Child Development. A key first step was to make teachers' learning about child development understandable and useful to them in the classroom. Although candidates were taking two courses about child development and learning in the psychology department, they were not able to connect what they were learning in these classes to what they were seeing in the classroom. As Professor Michael Ben-Avie noted,

> These courses were taught by psychology faculty members, and as a psychologist, I can say it was a weak approach. . . . Our discipline is organized in the worst possible way. We organize our discipline in terms of schools of thought instead of applications to student development and teaching.

Michael Ben-Avie and Norris Haynes, both of whom had been involved with the SDP, worked with the dean of the faculty at the time, Michael Sampson, to bring the faculty into discussion about how to make the teacher preparation more focused on what candidates needed to know for the classroom. Eventually, they replaced two courses from the psychology department with one course in the education department on Applied Child Development.

As is true in many other universities, a core component of this class is the child study, which is graded on a rubric informed by the SDP developmental pathways and guiding principles. This assignment is completed while candidates are in a student teaching placement—a feature of the program that was also changed. Ben-Avie explained, "Up until that point, in particular the field experiences, students made their own arrangements, and they could do the field experiences wherever they wanted, which most of the time was close to home. In general, that meant not in an urban area." The administration put in place a requirement that at least one student teaching or field experience needed to be in an urban setting. As Ben-Avie explained,

> We felt that the more that [teacher candidates] understood about child development applied in the classroom, and the more they picked the child that tugged at their hearts, and to follow, and to study, and to observe over time, the more they would really understand the students in the classroom.

Simply changing a course was a difficult exercise that took a committed faculty member with knowledge of the university's bureaucracy, as well as conversations with state policymakers, since the state of Connecticut requires preservice teachers to take certain coursework. As the university stewarded these changes, faculty members began to think more broadly about a collaborative that would root teacher candidates' experience more firmly in schools. They subsequently applied for a grant from the Kellogg Foundation. The Collaborative for Developmentally Centered Education was thus born, with the following objectives:

1. [To infuse] the needed knowledge and skills throughout preservice preparation, during the selection and induction process, and during professional development in ongoing school practice.
2. [To] prepare educators with the competencies to create environments and/or cultures that enable them to provide all students with a sense of belonging, being valued, and aspirations for success.
3. To engage district, state, and national authorities so that they can support integrated development and learning practices so that they become standard and sustained. (Comer, n.d.)

As part of the collaborative, key members from each of the three institutions (the university, the district, and Yale) meet quarterly as a full group to discuss common issues of practice. For the district, four schools are included, one of which is soon to become a university pilot school and will move to the SCSU campus.

This collaborative has already brought several changes. For example, the university's School of Social Work was included, and social work interns are now deployed to the four SDP schools. University faculty members interested in doing fieldwork have decided to conduct their research through the collaborative.

One unique aspect of the collaboration is the four-day summer academy, in which preservice students and veteran teachers learn together. The key objectives of the academy are to enable teachers to reflect on curriculum, instruction, relationships, and development; to reinforce the critical importance of the developmental pathways framework to guide and support instructional practices and interactions with students; and to provide participants with information, tools, and strategies that will help them integrate knowledge of child development into their existing practices.

The academy model of preservice and current teachers working together on a variety of learning activities over several days is a powerful one. Teacher candidates learn about applied child development theories, including aspects of neuroscience beyond what they are generally exposed to in their education courses. It also provides the opportunity for students to have in-depth discussions with, and learn from, current teachers. Even during student teaching, some preservice teachers are not afforded the chance to have such deep and meaningful discussions with their mentor teachers. The learning is mutual; participating teachers have expressed their appreciation for learning new ideas from prospective teachers.

This is important, Ben-Avie explained, because "during the course of the day-to-day work in schools, it's sometimes hard for the preservice teachers and the veteran teachers to really have time to sit together and talk." Preservice teachers continued this work by organizing seminars around topics they felt they still needed to know more about, such as special education. The goal is to identify issues "not in theory, and not about the disorder of the day, but in the classroom, what are the real issues that they need to deal with," noted Ben-Avie. "I think that's a way for them to identify gaps in their education."

The School of Education has also built a partnership with the School of Social Work so that social work interns would also be at the project schools learning alongside student teachers and veteran teachers in the collaborative framework of SDP, connecting to the Parent Team, the School Planning and Management Team, and—most important—the Student and Staff Support Team that provides services for students who are referred for additional supports.

Finally, the initiative is working to infuse the developmental principles that are part of the SDP into the Freedom School that is on campus during the summer and a new lab school that the university is launching as a site for student teaching, along with curriculum and school improvement work.

The collaboration among the university, the district, and the SDP offers other benefits to the schools. As school needs emerge, they can often be addressed by the university. For example, when Columbus School realized that it needed more help for teachers to better understand rigor and differentiation in the classroom, it accessed professors at Southern Connecticut to work with the faculty.

The university also helps the schools build on their strengths. When the Columbus principal realized that the school's 8th grade students were outperforming many of the high schools on a Spanish test, he thought, "Why don't we do an AP Spanish course at this school?" Because AP courses are not usually offered at middle schools, the SDP and the principal reached out to their partners at Southern Connecticut, including Professor Angela Lopez Vasquez, a bilingual education professor and member of the collaborative. She immediately met with the staff to figure out the requirements and the training needed to get the ball rolling.

As this account illustrates, the long-term prospects for a well-infused, developmentally supportive education throughout the district are strongly enhanced by this university-school partnership.

The Comer SDP and New Haven Public Schools: 50 Years of History

The story of the Comer Process in New Haven is as old as the story of the Comer Process itself. That New Haven is the home of the model has made its evolution there different than in any of the other places where the SDP has worked, according to Fay Brown:

> It's interesting—the Comer Model, in terms of its evolution in New Haven. It's different from any other places where we work because this is home. . . . All the other places where we have worked, it's been linear in terms of, you know, you go in, you do your contextual analysis, you work with the administrators, you work with the teachers, you spent three years or you spent five years, depending on the contract that you have with that district. And then you're out. In New Haven, we are here.

This extensive history between the Comer SDP and New Haven Public Schools, and the depth of the relationship that history has afforded, has helped to keep the process alive in the district's schools even through an era when most school districts forgot that focusing on the whole child could also help them support student achievement.

Over this long period, the adults in the system have learned how to work for students by more fully understanding who they are and what they need. In the words of Iline Tracey, "We are all working together. For what purpose? The service of students and their families. That makes so much sense to me. . . . When we're working with students; we need to understand them."

5

Creating and Sustaining Developmentally Grounded Education

~~~~~~~~~~~~~~~~~~~~~~~~~~~~~~

Reforming struggling schools is no easy task. Since the passage of No Child Left Behind in 2001, education policy has supported a notion of school accountability designed to shine a spotlight on schools that have struggled to achieve a very limited definition of success based on annual test score gains, label them "failing," and mete out a series of sanctions and punishments in an effort to inspire change. This punitive approach cascaded down through the education system: as schools were threatened with negative labels, staff reconstitutions, and closures, administrators often eliminated what were viewed as "frills"—arts, music, physical education, recess, science, social studies—and leaned on teachers to drive up scores.

Scripted curriculum and pacing guides were often used to push the curriculum through the standards at a rapid pace, with little opportunity for teachers to stop and pursue children's needs and interests or to listen to them about their lives outside school. As teachers managed these stresses, large numbers left high-needs schools, and others sought to remove students from class if they failed to learn easily or behaved poorly. Suspensions, expulsions, and referrals to special education soared in many communities serving low-income children (Losen & Gillespie, 2012; Vasquez Heilig & Darling-Hammond, 2008).

This narrow approach to education was ultimately unsuccessful in supporting meaningful gains in academic achievement. Although state test scores went up after the enactment of NCLB, as schools taught to multiple-choice tests measuring low-level skills and faced the threat of sanctions, national scores were largely flat and actually dropped at the end of the NCLB era; and U.S. performance on international tests measuring higher-order skills declined from 2000 to 2015 in math, reading, science, and problem solving (OECD, 2018). Furthermore, racial and economic gaps in achievement are 30 percent larger now than they were 30 years ago and greater in the United States than in most industrialized countries (Darling-Hammond, 2018).

In addition, the NCLB approach did not produce radical improvement in so-called low-performing schools. Some turnaround schools improved, but most did not (Gill, Timpane, Ross, Brewer, & Booker, 2007; Gleason, Clark, Tuttle, & Dwoyer, 2010). Others were closed and replaced by new schools that were often not more successful and that were replaced in turn by other schools (Davis & Raymond, 2012; Young et al., 2009). Charter schools, once heralded as a key method of school turnaround, have not proved to be a panacea; some do better than but more do the same as or worse than other public schools serving similar children. Furthermore, more than 2,500 charter schools were closed between 2001 and 2015—about 40 percent of all the charters launched in that time period. This instability creates additional problems for children, as those whose schools close abruptly experience a sense of abandonment and lower achievement than those who experience continuity in their education (NAACP, 2017).

The widening achievement and opportunity gap and the mandated reforms that have come along in the wake of the "failure" label have become an unfortunate snag in the fabric of education in the United States. Reforms, like fads, come and go; policymakers continue to find, try, and discard strategies and programs, trading "up" to the newest "thing" that promises the key to unlocking student achievement. This endless cycle has left many educators jaded and the general public distrustful, while too many students have continued to flounder, waiting for schools as an institution to figure out, on a grand scale, how to provide an education that will open windows of possibility and fulfill the promise of opportunity.

The School Development Program brings a very different theory of action from the one that existed during NCLB. Rather than using sanctions and punishments as motivators for change, the SDP uses knowledge and collaboration as motivators—assuming that parents and educators want to help children succeed and providing them with the knowledge to support child development and the tools to act collaboratively to create a village to raise each child.

The Every Student Succeeds Act (ESSA), adopted in 2015 as the successor to NCLB, encourages a more holistic conception of accountability. Within the more flexible policy landscape that has accompanied ESSA, schools are now better able to craft policies, enact practices, and use strategies that are more likely to develop students who feel a sense of purpose and connection to school, have transferable academic skills, graduate, and go on to college and productive careers at higher rates (Cook-Harvey, Darling-Hammond, Lam, Mercer, & Roc, 2016).

In this chapter we review some of the key lessons from the SDP experience and suggest recommendations for education practice and policy that can allow this kind of productive, developmentally grounded strategy to become the norm, rather than the exception, in U.S. education.

Lessons from the SDP Experience

Where the SDP achieved successful outcomes for students and schools, several elements were key: namely, relationship and culture building; professional and parent learning; attention to a wide range of data; district support; and empowerment, not punishment. In the following sections, we look at each of these in turn.

Relationship and culture building

Strong, trustful relationships are the foundation of successful school transformation. Among adults, these relationships can be built through mechanisms such as school teams and parent teams, provided they are accompanied by efforts to build collaboration and consensus-based decision making with a no-fault approach. Relationship-building activities are also important, including social occasions that simply build goodwill and familiarity among staff and parents, as well as specific outreach to parents through phone calls, home visits, and regular meetings. This approach allows faculty, staff, and parents to develop a collaborative, goal-oriented approach to transformation, willing to come together to do whatever it takes. Teachers' abilities to develop relationships with students are also strengthened as they have the opportunity to work within structures like advisories and looping that allow them to know students and their families well.

Professional and parent learning

Relationships between adults and children can also be strengthened as adults learn how to use affirmative supports for children's development, rather than punishment and exclusion. When parents and staff are both learning these kinds of strategies and engage in problem solving together, the combination creates a cohesive and supportive environment for children.

Ongoing professional development is essential. It is most effective when it is responsive to the needs that staff see in their practice and in their schools, when it is accompanied by facilitation and coaching by expert practitioners, and when there are opportunities for peer engagement and sharing of practices both within and across schools. Preservice preparation, especially in the context of school-university partnerships, strengthens these practices further, both by creating a pipeline of well-prepared teachers and by creating additional opportunities for shared professional learning within and across district schools.

Attention to a wide range of data

In successful SDP schools, staff learn to engage in data-driven decision making within a no-fault approach, focused on supporting students' developmental pathways and finding the root causes of any problems that have emerged. This analysis of data looks at all kinds of observational and quantitative information about children, their behaviors, and their learning, as well as information about teaching and school practices. Adults' abilities to understand these data and their implications for school, classroom, and individual practices drive successful problem solving and change.

District support

District support for this kind of practice includes support for professional learning and problem solving—for example, by funding professional development and providing key staff, such as district facilitators. Training district staff as well as school staff is important to develop a shared perspective on educational policy and practice grounded in child development, so that district approaches reinforce rather than contradict what schools are trying to do.

In addition, the district must understand its role in supporting schools to do their own, locally developed, context-specific improvements, rather than enforcing a compliance regimen or a standardized approach that does not permit schools to address the students they are serving or the problems they are seeking to solve. This suggests the need for some flexibility in decision making and in the use of resources at the school site, within parameters that are focused on the positive benefits to children.

Empowerment, not punishment

A key to success is that school and district leaders welcome input from teacher-leaders, parents, and students and help them feel empowered to make changes based on their growing knowledge, insights, and commitments to children's well-being. Schools must be able to make decisions based on their analyses of data, perceived needs, and goals for outcomes as reflected in the Comprehensive School Plan and the assessment and modification process. Doing so requires trust in professionals and parents and investments in their knowledge and efficacy.

Policies to Support Developmentally Grounded Education

These lessons suggest several areas of district, state, and federal policy that can support education that is more developmentally grounded. The experiences of Comer schools highlight six areas in particular that need policy supports: educator development, parent involvement, school redesign, Multi-Tiered Systems of Support (MTSS), transformed approaches to discipline, and accountability and continuous improvement systems.

Educator development

A clear lesson of the School Development Program is that educators—from administrators to teachers to support staff—need to understand how children develop if they are going to provide a rich and meaningful education. Schools participating in the Comer Process spend a significant amount of time educating their staff on the six developmental pathways. Often schools are trying to change ways of thinking—a difficult change process that takes time. Stronger preservice and inservice professional development efforts are needed to ensure that educators arrive at the school doors better prepared to support students, and that children, staff, and families' needs are continually addressed.

Preservice education

As Comer points out, "It's hard work to retrain people who've been in this field for a long time. It's better to train them correctly upfront before they're even in the field." The implication is that teacher preparation programs must embrace a focus on the full spectrum of child development. According to a report commissioned by the National Council for the Accreditation of Teacher Education (NCATE), "most educators...have not been prepared to apply knowledge of child and adolescent development and learning and are thus not sufficiently able to provide developmentally oriented instruction" (Snyder & Lit, 2010). Too often, teacher candidates are taught abstract concepts that are not directly tied to what they see and do in the classroom as student teachers, and later as practitioners.

The NCATE report suggests that teacher education programs should not only provide more formal opportunities to learn about child development in preservice coursework but also make sure that candidates' classroom experiences, from observations to student teaching, are organized in a way that allows candidates to reflect on and apply this approach in practice. Like the changes at Southern Connecticut State University described in Chapter 4, this can mean replacing courses in educational psychology that present abstract information about development and learning with courses on child or adolescent development that are designed to inform teaching decisions and are conducted in conjunction with fieldwork that makes that knowledge base vivid and applicable to classroom practice. A study of effective teacher preparation provides examples of how programs deeply grounded in child development and learning construct these kinds of courses (Darling-Hammond, 2006). Licensing and accreditation systems should focus more on teachers' learning opportunities and capacity to support child development and learning, to ensure that when teachers enter the classroom, they are well prepared to understand and teach children effectively.

Leader preparation is equally important. School principals and other administrators must understand child development and learning if they are to design schools that infuse this knowledge into school design, teaching, teacher development, school discipline, and parent involvement. Furthermore, leaders must learn how to develop authentic engagement from a wide range of stakeholders, embracing the principles of consensus, collaboration, and no-fault problem solving. Strong leadership is at the core of effective school development.

Another way to improve preservice education for both teachers and leaders is through university-school partnerships, which have been developed over time in the SDP (Comer et al., 1996). The partnership model involves shared ownership in which K–12 schools and institutions of higher education are active participants in school improvement and educator preparation. In the most recent example of SDP's university-district partnership between Southern Connecticut State University and New Haven School District, members of each institution meet regularly to discuss their ongoing needs. These conversations have led to modifications of the university's educator preparation programs, as well as inservice professional development and curriculum support for New Haven schools facilitated by university staff.

Inservice professional development

Sophisticated forms of teaching and leadership are needed to support and teach students along the six developmental pathways. In turn, effective professional development is needed to help teachers learn and refine the pedagogies required to support students in all of the ways that are important for their development and learning. Research shows that effective professional development meets several criteria: it is focused on content, incorporates active learning, supports collaboration in job-embedded contexts, uses modeling of effective practice, includes coaching and expert support, offers opportunity for feedback and reflection, and is of sustained duration (Darling-Hammond, Hyler, & Gardner, 2017).

The schools described in this book all relied upon an interactive process of reflection, evaluation, and action, which informed educators' collegial work and the kind of professional development they requested and, often, received. One theme that clearly emerges from the Comer schools is that professional development must be ongoing over the course of years, rather than following a "one-and-done" workshop model. Changing hearts and minds is a process that requires reflection, dialogue, and action that cannot happen in a single workshop. Furthermore, even in the highest-functioning schools, turnover is inevitable, and the needs of new staff must be continually addressed. For these reasons, policymakers and administrators must consider how to increase opportunities for deeper professional learning, such as professional learning communities, peer coaching, and collaborative planning, allocating appropriate funding and time in the school day for teachers, principals, and central office staff to work together.

Collaborative decision making can help ensure that professional development is designed to help meet students' actual developmental needs. "When the governance-management body is representative of all involved in the work of the school (parents, teachers, administrators), there is a clear and compelling mandate for self-development and for school development" (Comer, 1980). To take advantage of the motivation and insights provided by this process, administrators can routinely survey educators to identify professional learning needs. They can also develop the capacity and expertise of mentor teachers and coaches, who can provide valuable training to other educators.

Parent involvement

When students feel supported both at home and in school, student achievement improves. Students with involved parents have more self-confidence, feel school is more important, earn higher grades, and attend college (Henderson & Mapp, 2002). In a study of 100 Chicago schools, researchers found that parent involvement was a key ingredient for success, dramatically heightening the probability that schools would achieve growth in mathematics scores, motivation, and participation (Bryk, Sebring, Allensworth, Easton, &

Luppescu, 2010). Parent involvement has been consistently found to have significant, positive effects for children of color throughout the grades (Jeynes, 2012, 2017).

Creating parent partnerships

Because many parents have had negative experiences with schools themselves, especially in marginalized communities, schools must nurture strong staff-parent relationships by building in time and supports for teachers and advisors to engage parents as partners with valued expertise. In some communities where trust has been violated, it must be rebuilt in a proactive process that includes extensive listening, relationship building, and demonstrations that educators are trustworthy. School staff can engage parents as partners by planning teacher time for home visits, positive phone calls home, school meetings and student-teacher-parent conferences scheduled flexibly around parents' availability, as well as regular exchanges between home and school (Darling-Hammond, Ramos-Beban, Altamirano, & Hyler, 2016; Osher & Osher, 2002). States and districts should provide funding that supports teachers' time for these purposes, with the flexibility that allows them to be available when parents are available, not just during traditional school hours.

Training for parent engagement

To ensure that staff are equipped to work productively with families, they should be trained. However, teachers and administrators are rarely trained on how to work with parents, let alone given opportunities to practice building these relationships. Teachers and administrators would benefit from preservice and inservice training on building relationships with parents—for example, through simulated interviews, parent-teacher conferences, and working with parents in shared governance models (Comer, 1980). As is clear from the Comer Model, there should also be mechanisms through which parents can be engaged in the life of the school, through social events and parent education opportunities as well as through governance vehicles such as the Parent Team. These mechanisms should be accompanied by robust outreach to ensure that the parents involved in the school are representative of the diversity of the school. Some schools invite educators and parents to the same professional learning opportunities to enhance the partnership that can form from common goals and common knowledge.

School redesign

The SDP model is premised upon the belief that administrators, school staff, and parents must work together to ensure that every aspect of schooling is designed to foster child development. School and classroom structures should therefore "be designed to create and support strong attachments and positive, long-term relationships among adults and children that provide both academic and social-emotional support for cultivating developmentally appropriate skills, emotional security, resilience, and student agency" (Darling-Hammond et al., forthcoming). School-design features may include mechanisms for collaboration among staff, families, and the community, as the SDP demonstrates. Designs may also emphasize strategies to group students and adults so that strong relationships over a substantial period of time are possible.

Mechanisms for collaboration

Fundamental design features in the SDP are the mechanisms that promote collaboration among all participants. These include the School Planning and Management Team, the Student and Staff Support Team, and the Parent Team. Comer and colleagues argue that "schools' hierarchical management systems must be transformed into systems of collaboration and involvement of all the key stakeholders in the education of the children" (Comer et al., 1996).

Federal laws like the Every Student Succeeds Act include requirements for stakeholder engagement and school-site governance that includes parents. State and district policymakers and administrators can make sure that these are structured to be authentic opportunities for participation, rather than pro forma sign-offs on annual plans.

To make sure educators and parents are truly involved in the day-to-day operations of the school, opportunities for engagement should be routine. For teachers, this means having time built into the school day for collaboration and planning with one another and with support staff, such as school counselors and psychologists. For parents, there should be multiple opportunities for family engagement, ranging from participation in family conferences and events showcasing students' accomplishments to social gatherings that bring families and staff together. Such opportunities may also require redesign of school time and processes to make engagement possible and regular.

School structures that facilitate relationship building

School structures can be designed to facilitate relationship building. For example, an *advisory system* that focuses on relationship building is one structure that can work well in middle and high schools, where students have multiple courses with multiple teachers. In advisory systems, each teacher advises and serves as an advocate for a small group of students that meets regularly over two to four years to support academic progress and create a sense of community. Advisory is an important feature in some Comer schools (Noblit, Malloy, & Malloy, 2001). A parallel structure used in many Comer elementary schools, including those in New Haven, is the *morning meeting*, in which teachers start the day facilitating a greeting and team-building activity (Comer, Ben-Avie, Haynes, & Joyner, 1999). The meeting serves as a way for students and teachers to get to know one another, start the day on the right foot, and practice the SDP guiding principles.

Grade-level looping, the practice of having a teacher stay with the same group of students over two or more years, also facilitates relationship building and was used in schools such as Weir Elementary in New Jersey. Continuity with an educator and a group of students can foster strong relationships and allow teachers to understand their students' needs more deeply, and it has been associated with higher academic achievement, particularly for children who struggle academically (Bogart, 2002; Hampton, Mumford, & Bond, 1998).

Small schools and class sizes, which are the focus of some school redesign efforts, allow educators to know their students and families more effectively. Small schools and school learning communities have been shown to improve secondary school students' achievement and graduation rates (Darling-Hammond, Ross, & Milliken, 2007). Small class sizes have been shown to have important benefits, especially for young children, children from low-income families, and those who have struggled in school (Glass & Smith, 1979; Kim, 2006/2007; Mosteller, 1995). These design features make it possible to respond to children's developmental needs if knowledge of those needs and strategies to support them is present.

Multi-Tiered Systems of Support

Much of what the SDP has done to identify and meet students' needs is captured in what today is being characterized as Multi-Tiered Systems of Support (MTSS) that help educators figure out what students need and how to make supports more readily available. Students who are experiencing poverty and toxic stress (Shonkoff et al., 2012) have additional needs that are not typically addressed in K–12 schools. These children often need early childhood education, health and mental health supports, and social services to promote their healthy development. Integrated student supports in schools, often called wraparound services, can help schools address barriers to learning and improve attendance, academic achievement, and student behavior when well implemented (Oakes, Maier, & Daniel, 2017).

Early childhood education

Early care and education (ECE) is the foundation for child development, setting the stage for the social, emotional, and academic learning needed for later life success. High-quality early childhood education has consistently demonstrated large, strong effects on later success in school and life (Yoshikawa et al., 2013). But for many families, high-quality ECE is out of reach; the average cost of center-based infant care equals more than a quarter of a median income in most states (Child Care Aware, 2017). Thus, many children enter school without this support.

One example of how early learning can be well integrated with K–12 schools is the Comer-Zigler (CoZi) project, a collaboration that brings child care and family support services together with elementary schools. It provides full-day care for preschool age children, as well as support and guidance for pregnant women and families with children under age 3. As described in Chapter 2, demonstration projects showed early evidence of success. In addition to supporting children's development, they also provide important financial and stress relief for parents, in some cases freeing parents up to be more active participants in schools or pursue their own education or careers (Finn-Stevenson & Stern, 1997).

Some states have developed effective universal preschool programs (Wechsler et al., 2016), and others have begun to expand the reach and quality of their programs. This is an area of developmental support that states and cities can undertake with significant returns on investment in terms of less money spent on grade retention, special education placements, remediation, dropouts, and incarceration, and greater returns in the form of employment and higher wages later in life (Levin, 2009).

Health, mental health, and social services

School districts and policymakers can also take important steps toward ensuring that students have access to the health, mental health, and social services they need through their schools. When these services are coordinated with the school system, "the mission of the school changes from being only the purveyor of knowledge to being a central, coalescing agent where vital services for children and families are provided in an integrated way" (Comer et al., 1996, p. 23). In all SDP schools, social workers, psychologists, and other mental health professionals are involved in planning for student success. Some schools have gone several steps further by bringing health and dental care to their schools' campuses.

In addition to providing services, professionals offering supplemental services should be involved in the daily life of the school, attending student support meetings, supporting families, and working with educators. For example, in Cleveland's SDP, where the Cleveland Child Guidance Center provides mental health services to children and their families, clinicians also provide mental health consultation to teachers and co-construct a plan for the children with whom they work (Klein, cited in Comer et al., 1996). If robust collaboration is to take place, schools must be staffed with a sufficient number of social workers, psychologists, and other professionals in order to allow sufficient time to dedicate to each student. In many cases, schools have had to raise their own funds to ensure the availability of vital services, many of which can save taxpayers money by providing children with preventative care and avoiding expensive emergency room visits for nonurgent care.

Policymakers can help fund these programs or provide an incentive for collaboration with local health care providers. A new set of initiatives for community schools that provide such services in a collaborative framework has been undertaken by states and cities with significant success; these can provide policy models for others (Oakes et al., 2017).

Transformed approaches to discipline

Research indicates that over the last several decades, the overuse and disparate use of suspensions and expulsions have been significant contributors to student exclusion and school failure as well as higher dropout rates and the perpetuation of the school-to-prison pipeline.

These high rates of student exclusion have been encouraged by zero-tolerance policies, which assign explicit, predetermined punishments to specific violations of school rules, regardless of the situation or context of the behavior (American Psychological Association, 2008). Students who are removed from school lose instructional time and tend to have lower rates of academic success, higher rates of grade retention, and lower graduation rates, and they are more likely to become involved in the juvenile justice system (Steinberg & Lacoe, 2017).

A major reason for this harsh and counterproductive approach to discipline, suggests Comer, is that educators and even some mental health professionals are not adequately trained in child development and developmentally appropriate practices, which makes it difficult for them to understand or learn why children act as they do, how adults influence this behavior, and what supports can enable positive behavior.

Revising exclusionary district discipline policies

The SDP uses a developmental approach in interacting with children that helps educators understand the root cause of children's behaviors and address trauma, anxiety, or lack of knowledge of better conflict-resolution or problem-solving strategies. To reduce suspension and expulsion rates, as well as disciplinary disparities by race and gender, states, districts, and schools should remove zero-tolerance policies and eliminate the use of suspensions and expulsions for lower-level offenses, replacing them with diagnostic and restorative strategies to address student needs and misbehavior. In addition, states and districts can support the development and implementation of model school discipline policies. (See Cardichon & Darling-Hammond, 2017, for resources for such strategies, training, and policies.)

Training the school community in educative and restorative approaches

Schools that have traditionally relied upon zero-tolerance policies will need support in making the transition to a new approach.

Schools will benefit from offering explicit training in restorative practices, social-emotional learning, and other positive approaches to discipline, especially since they run counter to the approaches many educators have learned or were taught themselves.

Hundreds of studies have established the effectiveness of social-emotional learning programs in improving student behavior, school climate, and school safety, and have found that—by creating a better context for learning—they increase student achievement as well (Durlak et al., 2011). States, districts, and schools can identify and provide strong training, and they can support educators in the learning process with time and coaching for professional learning and facilitators for adult- and peer-mediation strategies that often accompany such approaches.

The SDP does not specify a disciplinary policy, yet many SDP schools have established practices that build social-emotional learning and include features like *restorative justice*, an approach that emphasizes repairing the harm caused by problematic behavior. It is generally accomplished through cooperative processes that include all stakeholders, leading to transformation of people, relationships, and communities. In schools, restorative justice programs bring the affected parties together to evaluate the situation, determine how to make amends, and reintegrate students into the classroom and school community (Davis, 2015).

Accountability and continuous improvement systems

Despite the American promise of equal educational opportunity for all students, persistent achievement gaps between more and less advantaged groups of students remain. Although NCLB drew attention to this pernicious problem, the accountability system's exclusive focus on math and reading scores led to an emphasis on a narrow slice of students' cognitive development, at the expense of a broader view of development. Furthermore, it mandated top-down, punitive reform, which undermined the focus on no-fault, collaborative decision making needed to make lasting and effective school change.

Broader indicators of school success

The Every Student Succeeds Act provides states with an opportunity to implement higher-quality accountability and improvement systems that include multiple measures of school success—measures that will help determine what issues garner state and local attention, what school practices come with an incentive, and what policies and supports are provided to ensure that student needs are addressed. As states and districts develop their accountability and improvement systems, they can choose high-leverage measures of school progress that, when combined with effective policies, hold promise for supporting success for the youth most marginalized by the education system. States, districts, and schools can choose to do the following:

- Evaluate school climate—for example, with school-climate surveys or walkthrough protocols that provide schools with much needed information about where they are succeeding and where they can improve.
- Track suspension and expulsion rates, an important indicator of exclusionary disciplinary practices that schools should seek to remedy.
- Monitor attendance and chronic absenteeism so that these will be a focus of schools' attention.
- Use an extended-year graduation rate (e.g., five- and six-year rates), as well as a four-year rate, to encourage high schools to work with and bring back young people who, for a variety of reasons, could not graduate in four years.
- Examine the richness of student curriculum opportunities, including access to college- and career-ready courses and programs (Cardichon & Darling-Hammond, 2017).

Individual schools in the SDP have been using these measures to evaluate their own progress for years and to identify problems and successes (see Comer, 1980; Noblit et al., 2001). These measures are strong predictors of student success and distinguishers of equitable opportunities; and when used to support ongoing data, they can encourage productive improvement in schools and districts (Cardichon & Darling-Hammond, 2017).

A number of states have begun to use these kinds of broader measures of school success under ESSA and to support schools in devising the developmental, restorative, parent-outreach, and curricular practices that can support improvement. Having a broad focus on these multiple measures of school success can support schools in collecting, analyzing, and acting upon these data in ways that transform education for students.

Support for continuous improvement

States and districts can also support continuous improvement by providing not only useful data but also related professional development supports for school learning. Research on the Comer schools demonstrates that changing schools is a lengthy, complex process that often requires significant resources and collaboration. State policymakers and districts should ensure that schools have access to the funding and expertise they need to analyze outcome data, identify organizational changes that need to be made, implement high-quality professional development, and support students' development along multiple pathways.

Schools may need supports such as technical assistance, facilitation of peer-learning networks, and funding for professional development for educators and community members. States and districts can additionally reach out to families and communities to understand their priorities and what they think is needed to support students. As the Comer Model stresses, a diverse array of stakeholders should be included so all parties can work together to support children's development.

Conclusion

In the final analysis, a developmentally supportive approach to education benefits not only the students who are more humanely and productively taught and parented but also the society as a whole—as support for students translates into their ability to contribute in many ways to their families and communities. As John Dewey (1907) reminded us,

> What the best and wisest parent wants for his or her child, that must the community want for all of its children. Any other goal is narrow and unlovely. Acted upon, it destroys our democracy. . . . Only by being true to the full growth of all the individuals who make it up, can society by any chance be true to itself. (p. 19)

References

American Psychological Association Zero Tolerance Task Force. (2008). Are zero tolerance policies effective in schools? An evidentiary review and recommendations. *American Psychologist, 63*(9), 852–862.

ASCD. (n.d.). Whole child approach. www.ascd.org/whole-child.aspx

Bass, P. (2009, September 28). "Comer" is back. *New Haven Independent.* Retrieved from www.newhavenindependent.org/index.php/archives/entry/comer_is_back

Berkowitz, R., Moore, H., Astor, R. A., & Benbenishty, R. (2016). A research synthesis of the associations between socioeconomic background, inequality, school climate, and academic achievement. *Review of Educational Research, 87*(2), 425–469.

Bloom, H. S., & Unterman, R. (2014). Can small high schools of choice improve educational prospects for disadvantaged students? *Journal of Policy Analysis and Management, 33*(2), 290–319.

Bogart, V. S. (2002). *The effects of looping on the academic achievement of elementary school students.* (Doctoral dissertation). Retrieved from Digital Commons @ East Tennessee State University, http://dc.etsu.edu/etd/707

Borman, G. D., Hewes, G. M., Overman, L. T., & Brown, S. (2003). Comprehensive school reform and student achievement: A meta-analysis. *Review of Educational Research, 73*(2), 125–230.

Brown, F. E., & Murray, E. T. (2005). Essentials of literacy: From a pilot site at Davis Street School to district-wide intervention. *Journal of Education for Students Placed at Risk 10*(2): 185–197.

Bryk, A. S., & Schneider, B. (2002). *Trust in schools: A core resource for improvement.* New York: Russell Sage Foundation.

Bryk, A. S., Sebring, P. B., Allensworth, E., Easton, J. Q., & Luppescu, S. (2010). *Organizing schools for improvement: Lessons from Chicago.* Chicago: University of Chicago Press.

Cantor, P., Osher, D., Berg, J., Steyer, L., & Rose, T. (2018). Malleability, plasticity, and individuality: How children learn and develop in context. *Applied Developmental Science.*

Cardichon, J., & Darling-Hammond, L. (2017). Advancing educational equity for underserved youth: How new state accountability systems can support school inclusion and student success. Palo Alto, CA: Learning Policy Institute. https://learningpolicyinstitute.org/product/advancing-educational-equity-underserved-youth-report

Center on the Developing Child at Harvard University. (2016). *From best practices to breakthrough impacts: A science-based approach to building a more promising future for young children and families.* Cambridge, MA: Harvard University, Center on the Developing Child.

Child Care Aware. (2017). Parents and the high cost of care. Retrieved from https://usa.childcareaware.org/wp-content/uploads/2017/12/2017_CCA_High_Cost_Report_FINAL.pdf

Cohen, D. J., & Solnit, A. J. (1996). Foreword. In J. P. Comer, N. M. Haynes, E. T. Joyner, & M. Ben-Avie (Eds.), *Rallying the whole village: The Comer process for reforming education* (pp. xi–xvi). New York: Teachers College Press.

Comer, J. P. (n.d.). Unpublished concept paper for the Kellogg Foundation. Received March 26, 2018, via personal communication.

Comer, J. P. (1980). *School power: Implications of an intervention project.* New York: The Free Press.

Comer, J. P. (1988). Educating poor minority children. *Scientific American, 259*(5), 42–49.

Comer, J. P. (1992, Winter). Opening the door to learning. *Agenda,* 26–28.

Comer, J. P. (1992–93, Winter). Educational accountability: A shared responsibility between parents and schools. *Stanford Law & Policy Review,* 113–122.

Comer, J. P., Ben-Avie, M., Haynes, N. M., & Joyner, E. T. (Eds.). (1999). *Child by child: The Comer process for change in education.* New York: Teachers College Press.

Comer, J. P., & Emmons, C. (2006, Summer). The research program of the Yale Child Study Center School Development Program. *Journal of Negro Education, 75*(3), 353–372.

Comer, J. P., Giordano, L., & Brown, F. E. (2012). Case Study 13A: Integrating six developmental pathways in the classroom: The synergy between teacher and students. In P. M. Brown, M. W. Corrigan, & A. Higgins-D'Allesandro (Eds.), *Handbook of Prosocial Education, Vol. 2* (pp. 445–458). Lanham, MD: Rowman & Littlefield.

Comer, J. P., & Haynes, N. M. (1991). Parent involvement in schools: An ecological approach. *Elementary School Journal, 91*(3), 271–277.

Comer, J. P., Haynes, N. M., Joyner, E. T., & Ben-Avie, M. (Eds.). (1996). *Rallying the whole village: The Comer process for reforming education.* New York: Teachers College Press.

Comer, J. P., Joyner, E. T., & Ben-Avie, M. (Eds.). (2004). *Six pathways to healthy child development and academic success: The field guide to Comer schools in action.* Thousand Oaks, CA: Corwin Press.

Comer, J. P., & Savo, C. (2009). *Focused on development: The Davis Street Interdistrict Magnet School in New Haven, Connecticut.* [Video recording]. New Haven, CT: School Development Program, Yale Child Study Center.

Comer School Program. (n.d.). Retrieved from https://medicine.yale.edu/childstudy/ communitypartnerships/comer

Cook, T. D., Habib, F. N., Phillips, M., Settersten, R. A., Shagle, S. C., & Degirmencio-glu, S. M. (1999). Comer's school development program in Prince George's County, Maryland: A theory-based evaluation. *American Educational Research Journal, 36*(3), 543–597.

Cook, T. D., Murphy, R. F., & Hunt, H. D. (2000). Comer's School Development Program in Chicago: A theory-based evaluation. *American Educational Research Journal, 37*(2), 535–597.

Cook-Harvey, C., Darling-Hammond, L., Lam, L., Mercer, C., & Roc, M. (2016). *Equity and ESSA: Leveraging educational opportunity through the Every Student Succeeds Act.* Palo Alto, CA: Learning Policy Institute.

Darling-Hammond, L. (2006). *Powerful teacher education: Lessons from exemplary programs.* San Francisco: Jossey-Bass.

Darling-Hammond, L. (2007). Race, inequality, and educational accountability: The irony of "No Child Left Behind." *Race, Ethnicity, and Education, 10*(3), 245–260.

Darling-Hammond, L. (2010). *The flat world and education: How America's commitment to equity will determine our future.* New York: Teachers College Press.

Darling-Hammond, L. (2018). *Education and the path to one nation, indivisible.* Palo Alto, CA: Learning Policy Institute.

Darling-Hammond, L., Cook-Harvey, C., Flook, L., Barron, B., & Osher, D. (forthcoming). Science of learning and development: Implications for educational practice. *Applied Developmental Science.*

Darling-Hammond, L., Hyler, M. E., & Gardner, M. (2017). *Effective teacher professional development.* Palo Alto, CA: Learning Policy Institute.

Darling-Hammond, L., Ramos-Beban, N., Altamirano, R., & Hyler, M. (2016). *Be the change: Reinventing school for student success.* New York: Teachers College Press.

Darling-Hammond, L., Ross, P., & Milliken, M. (2007). High school size, organization, and content: What matters for student success? In F. Hess (Ed.), *Brookings Papers on Education Policy, 2006/07* (pp. 163–204). Washington, DC: Brookings Institution Press.

Datnow, A., Borman, G. D., Stringfield, S., Overman, L. T., & Castellano, M. (2003). Comprehensive school reform in culturally and linguistically diverse contexts:

Implementation and outcomes from a four-year study. *Educational Evaluation and Policy Analysis, 25*(2), 143–170.

Davis, D. H., & Raymond, M. E. (2012). Choices for studying choice: Assessing charter school effectiveness using two quasi-experimental methods. *Economics of Education Review, 31*(2), 225–236.

Davis, M. (2015). Restorative justice: Resources for schools. Retrieved from www. edu- topia.org/blog/restorative-justice-resources-matt-davis

Desimone, L., Finn-Stevenson, M., & Henrich, C. (2000). Whole school reform in a low-income African American community: The effects of the CoZi model on teachers, parents, and students. *Urban Education, 35*(3), 269–323.

Dewey, J. (1907). *The school and society.* Chicago: University of Chicago Press.

Dryfoos, J. G. (2000). Evaluation of community schools: Findings to date. Washington, DC: Coalition for Community Schools. Retrieved from www.community-schools.org/assets/1/AssetManager/Evaluation%20of%20Community%20Schools_joy_dryfoos.pdf

Durlak, J. A., Weissberg, R. P., Dymnicki, A. B., Taylor, R. D., & Schellinger, K. B. (2011). The impact of enhancing students' social and emotional learning: A meta-analysis of school-based universal interventions. *Child Development, 82*(1), 405–432.

Emmons, C. L., & Baskerville, R. (2005). Maintaining excellence while managing transitions: Norman S. Weir revisited. *Journal of Education for Students Placed at Risk, 10*(2), 199–207.

Emmons, C. L., Efimba, M. O., & Hagopian, G. (1998). A school transformed: The case of Norman S. Weir. *Journal of Education for Students Placed at Risk, 3*(1): 39–51.

Felner, R. D., Seitsinger, A. M., Brand, S., Burns, A., & Bolton, N. (2007). Creating small learning communities: Lessons from the project on high-performing learning communities about "what works" in creating productive, developmentally enhancing learning contexts. *Educational Psychologist, 42*(4), 209–221.

Finn-Stevenson, F., & Stern, B. M. (1997). Integrating early-childhood and family-support services with a school improvement process: The Comer-Zigler Initiative. *Elementary School Journal, 98*(1), 51–66.

Friedlaender, D., Burns, D., Lewis-Charp, H., Cook-Harvey, C. M., & Darling-Hammond, L. (2014). *Student-centered schools: Closing the opportunity gap.* Palo Alto, CA: Stanford Center for Opportunity Policy in Education.

Garriga, M. (2005, July 31). Old ideas look new again as test-score gap widens. *New Haven Independent.* Retrieved from www.nhregister.com/news/article/Old-ideas-look-new-again-as-test-score-gap-widens-11644111.php

Gill, B., Timpane, P. M., Ross, K. E., Brewer, D. J., & Booker, K. (2007). *Rhetoric versus reality: What we know and what we need to know about vouchers and charter schools.* Santa Monica, CA: RAND Corporation.

Glass, G. V., & Smith, M. (1979). Meta-analysis of class size and achievement. *Educational Evaluation and Policy Analysis, 1*(1), 2–16.

Gleason, P., Clark, M., Tuttle, C. C., & Dwoyer, E. (2010). *The evaluation of charter school impacts: Final report* [NCEE 2010-4029]. Washington, DC: U.S. Department of Education, Institute of Education Sciences, National Center for Education Evaluation and Regional Assistance.

Hampton, F. M., Mumford, D. A., & Bond, L. (1998). Parent involvement in inner-city schools: The project FAST extended family approach to success. *Urban Education, 33*(3), 410–427.

Haynes, N. M., & Comer, J. P. (1990). The effects of a school development program on self-concept. *Yale Journal of Biology and Medicine, 63*(4), 275.

Haynes, N. M., & Comer, J. P. (1993). The Yale School Development Program: Process, outcomes, and policy implications. *Urban Education, 28*(2), 166–199.

Haynes, N. M., Comer, J. P., & Hamilton-Lee, M. (1989). School climate enhancement through parental involvement. *Journal of School Psychology, 27*(1), 87–90.

Haynes, N. M., Emmons, C. L., & Woodruff, D. W. (1998). School Development Program effects: Linking implementation to outcomes. *Journal of Education for Students Placed at Risk, 3*(1), 71–85.

Henderson, A. T., & Mapp, K. L. (2002). A new wave of evidence: The impact of school, family and community connections on student achievement. Austin, TX: National Center for Family & Community Connections with Schools.

Jennings, P. A., & Greenberg, M. T. (2009). The prosocial classroom: Teacher social and emotional competence in relation to student and classroom outcomes. *Review of Educational Research, 79*(1), 491–525.

Jeynes, W. H. (2012). A meta-analysis of the efficacy of different types of parental involvement programs for urban students. *Urban Education, 47*(4), 706–742.

Jeynes, W. H. (2017). A meta-analysis: The relationship between parental involvement and Latino student outcomes. *Education and Urban Society, 49*(1), 4–28.

Jones, S. M., & Bouffard, S. M. (2012). Social and emotional learning in schools: From programs to strategies. *Social Policy Report, 26*(4).

Joyner, E. T., Ben-Avie, M., & Comer, J. P. (2004). *Transforming school leadership and management to support student learning and development: The field guide to Comer schools in action.* Thousand Oaks, CA: Corwin Press.

Kim, J. (2006/2007). The relative influence of research on class-size policy. *Brookings Papers on Education Policy,* 273–295. Washington, DC: Brookings Institution Press.

Ladd, H. F. (2001). School-based educational accountability systems: The promise and the pitfalls. *National Tax Journal, 54*(2), 385–400.

Lee, V. E., Bryk, A. S., & Smith, J. B. (1993). Chapter 5: The organization of effective secondary schools. *Review of Research in Education, 19*(1), 171–267.

LePage, P., Darling-Hammond, L., Akar, H. (2005). Classroom management. In L. Darling-Hammond & J. Bransford (Eds.), *Preparing teachers for a changing world: What teachers should learn and be able to do* (pp. 327–357). San Francisco: Wiley.

Levin, H. (2009). The economic payoff to investing in educational justice. *Educational Researcher, 38*(1), 5–20.

Losen, D. J., & Gillespie, J. (2012). Opportunities suspended: The disparate impact of disciplinary exclusion from school. Retrieved from www.civilrightsproject.ucla.edu/resources/projects/center-for-civil-rights-remedies/school-to-prison-folder/federal-reports/upcoming-ccrr-research/losen-gillespie-opportunity-suspended-2012.pdf

Lunenburg, F. C. (2011, December). The Comer School Development Program: Improving education for low-income students. *National Forum of Multicultural Issues Journal, 8*(1).

MacInnes, G. (2009). *In plain sight: Simple, difficult lessons from New Jersey's efforts to close the achievement gap.* New York: Century Foundation.

Maier, A., Daniel, J., Oakes, J., & Lam, L. (2017). *Community schools as an effective school improvement strategy: A review of the evidence.* Palo Alto, CA: Learning Policy Institute.

Melnick, H., Cook-Harvey, C. M., & Darling-Hammond, L. (2017). *Encouraging social and emotional learning in the context of new accountability.* Palo Alto, CA: Learning Policy Institute. Retrieved from http://learningpolicyinstitute.org/product/sel-new-accountability

Mosteller, F. (1995). The Tennessee study of class size in the early school grades. *The Future of Children, 5*(2), 113–127.

National Association for the Advancement of Colored People (NAACP). (2017). *Quality education for all: One school at a time.* Baltimore, MD: NAACP. Retrieved from www.naacp.org/wp-content/uploads/2017/07/Task_ForceReport_final2.pdf

National School Climate Center (NSCC). (n.d.). Shared leadership across contexts. www.schoolclimate.org/climate

National Scientific Council on the Developing Child. (2010). Persistent fear and anxiety can affect young children's learning and development: Working Paper No. 9. Retrieved from www.developingchild.net

New Haven Public Schools. (n.d. a). NHPS school change & district improvement plan. Retrieved April 6, 2018, from www.nhps.net/sites/default/files/School_Change_diagram.pdf

New Haven Public Schools. (n.d. b). NHPS school climate survey. Retrieved April 6, 2018, from www.nhps.net/climate

New Haven Public Schools. (n.d. c). Unified Code of Conduct 2016-2017. Retrieved April 6, 2018, from www.nhps.net/sites/default/files/2016-17_Code_of_Conduct.pdf

Noblit, G. W., Malloy, W. W., & Malloy, C. E. (Eds.). (2001). *The kids got smarter: Case studies of successful Comer schools*. Cresskill, NJ: Hampton Press.

Oakes, J., Maier, A., & Daniel, J. (2017). Community schools: An evidence-based strategy for equitable school improvement. Boulder, CO: National Education Policy Center. Retrieved from http://nepc.colorado.edu/publication/equitable-community-schools

Olson. (2017). *Science of learning and development: Summary*. Unpublished manuscript.

Organisation for Economic Co-operation and Development (OECD). (2018). *PISA 2015: Results in focus*. Paris: OECD.

Osher, D., Cantor, P., Berg, J., Steyer, L., & Rose, T. (2018). Drivers of human development: How relationships and context shape learning and development. *Applied Developmental Science*, 1–31.

Osher, T. W., & Osher, D. M. (2002). The paradigm shift to true collaboration with families. *Journal of Child and Family Studies, 11*(1), 47–60.

Peak, C. (2018, March 26). Martinez School phases out suspensions. *New Haven Independent*. Retrieved from www.newhavenindependent.org/index.php/archives/entry/martinez_social_emotional_learning_behavior

Rumberger, R. W. (2012, January 24). America cannot afford the stiff price of a dropout nation. Retrieved from http://theeducatedguess.org/2012/01/24/america-cannot-afford-the-stiff-price-of-a-dropout-nation

Shelton, J. (2014, February 24). From New Haven to the White House, Comer's message of academic excellence endures. *New Haven Register*. Retrieved from http://nhregister.com/colleges/article/From-New-Haven-to-the-White-House-Comer-s-11381477.php

Shonkoff, J. P., Garner, A. S., Siegel, B. S., Dobbins, M. I., Earls, M. F., McGuinn, L., . . . & Committee on Early Childhood, Adoption, and Dependent Care. (2012). The lifelong effects of early childhood adversity and toxic stress. *Pediatrics, 129*(1), e232–e246.

Smith, A. (2011, May 16). Blumenthal visits New Haven school to learn about successful education strategies. *New Haven Register*. Retrieved April 6, 2018, from www.nhregister.com/news/article/Blumenthal-visits-New-Haven-school-to-learn-about-11561404.php

Snyder, J., & Lit, I. (2010). Principles and exemplars for integrating developmental sciences knowledge into educator preparation. Washington, DC: National Council for Accreditation of Teacher Education.

Steinberg, M. P., & Lacoe, J. (2017). What do we know about school discipline reform? *Education Next, 17*(1), 1–23.

Vasquez Heilig, J., & Darling-Hammond, L. (2008). Accountability Texas style: The progress and learning of urban minority students in a high-stakes testing context. *Educational Evaluation and Policy Analysis, 30*(2), 75–110.

Wald, J., & Losen, D. J. (2003). Defining and redirecting a school-to-prison pipeline. *New Directions for Youth Development, 2003*(99), 9–15.

Wechsler, M., Kirp, D., Tinubu Ali, T., Gardner, M., Maier, A., Melnick, H., & Shields, P. (2016). *The road to high-quality early learning: Lessons from the states.* Washington, DC: Learning Policy Institute.

Yoshikawa, H., Weiland, C., Brooks-Gunn, J., Burchinal, M. R., Espinosa, L. M., Gormley, et al. (2013). *Investing in our future: The evidence base on preschool education.* Ann Arbor, MI: Society for Research in Child Development.

Young, V. M., Humphrey, D. C., Wang, H., Bosetti, K. R., Cassidy, L., Wechsler, M. E., et al. (2009). *Renaissance schools fund-supported schools: Early outcomes, challenges, and opportunities.* Menlo Park, CA: Stanford Research International and Chicago Consortium on Chicago School Research.

Index

The letter *f* following a page number denotes a figure.

About the Authors

Linda Darling-Hammond is president of the Learning Policy Institute and the Charles E. Ducommun Professor of Education Emeritus at Stanford University, where she founded the Stanford Center for Opportunity Policy in Education and served as the faculty sponsor of the Stanford Teacher Education Program, which she helped to redesign.

Darling-Hammond is past president of the American Educational Research Association and recipient of its awards for Distinguished Contributions to Research, Lifetime Achievement, and Research-to-Policy. She is also a member of the American Association of Arts and Sciences and of the National Academy of Education. From 1994 to 2001, she was executive director of the National Commission on Teaching and America's Future, whose 1996 report *What Matters Most: Teaching for America's Future* was named one of the most influential reports affecting U.S. education in that decade. In 2006, Darling-Hammond was named one of the nation's 10 most influential people affecting educational policy. In 2008, she served as the leader of President Barack Obama's education policy transition team.

Darling-Hammond began her career as a public school teacher and cofounded both a preschool and a public high school. Among her more than 500 publications are a number of award-winning books, including *The Right to Learn, Teaching as the Learning Profession, Preparing Teachers for a Changing World,* and *The Flat World and Education.*

Channa M. Cook-Harvey is the director of social and emotional learning at Folsom Cordova Unified School District. In collaboration with Instructional Services and Special Education, she is working to strengthen FCUSD's efforts to educate the whole child. In this role, she provides leadership, planning, coordination, and management to support the development of infrastructure that creates the conditions, culture, and competencies to guide social-emotional learning districtwide.

Previously, Cook-Harvey was a senior researcher at the Learning Policy Institute in Palo Alto, CA. There, she collaborated with colleagues to lead, design, and manage complex national and California-based qualitative education research studies focused on social-emotional learning, whole child approaches to schooling, and trauma-informed practices. She began her career in education as a high school English teacher and literacy coach in Los Angeles Unified School District, and she cofounded and served as principal of a charter school in New Orleans.

Lisa Flook holds a PhD in (Clinical) Psychology from UCLA. She is a senior researcher at the Learning Policy Institute, involved in translating research on children's learning and development to inform practice and policy. She has conducted research in educational settings for over 15 years. Her earlier research focused on the negative consequences of academic and interpersonal stress on children and adolescents. A strong interest in prevention and intervention led her to investigate approaches to mitigate the negative effects of stress and to promote health and well-being starting in childhood. She has studied the effects of mindfulness in school settings at UCLA's Mindful Awareness Research Center and at the Center for Healthy Minds at the University of Wisconsin-Madison.

Madelyn Gardner is a research and policy associate at the Learning Policy Institute. There, she has conducted research on issues of access and quality in state early learning systems and on effective preparation and development of teachers and school leaders. Previously, Gardner worked at the Next Generation think tank, where she supported evidence-based children and family policy development in California, and taught English as a foreign language at Payap University in Thailand. She holds an MA in International Education Policy from Stanford University.

Hanna Melnick is a research analyst and policy advisor at the Learning Policy Institute, where she coleads the Early Childhood Learning team. Her research there has focused on school climate, social and emotional learning, accountability, and building effective early learning systems. Previously, Melnick conducted research on California's Local Control Funding Formula and early learning systems. She began her career in education as an elementary teacher. Melnick holds an MPP from the Goldman School of Public Policy at UC Berkeley and received her BA from Harvard University.

Related ASCD Resources

At the time of publication, the following resources were available (ASCD stock numbers in parentheses).

Print Products

Building Equity: Policies and Practices to Empower All Learners by Dominique Smith, Nancy E. Frey, Ian Pumpian, and Douglas E. Fisher (#117031)

Challenging the Whole Child: Reflections on Best Practices in Learning, Teaching, and Leadership edited by Marge Scherer and the Educational Leadership Staff (#109114E4)

Engaging the Whole Child: Reflections on Best Practices in Learning, Teaching, and Leadership edited by Marge Scherer and the Educational Leadership Staff (#109103E4)

Leading with Focus: Elevating the Essentials for School and District Improvement by Mike Schmoker (#116024)

Fighting for Change in Your School: How to Avoid Fads and Focus on Substance by Harvey Alvy (#117007)

Keeping the Whole Child Healthy and Safe: Reflections on Best Practices in Learning, Teaching, and Leadership edited by Marge Scherer and the Educational Leadership Staff (#110130E4

Leading Change Together: Developing Educator Capacity Within Schools and Systems by Eleanor Drago-Severson and Jessica Blum-DeStefano (#117027)

Supporting the Whole Child: Reflections on Best Practices in Learning, Teaching, and Leadership edited by Marge Scherer and the Educational Leadership Staff (#110058E4)

Transformational Teaching in the Information Age: Making Why and How We Teach Relevant to Students by Thomas R. Rosebrough and Ralph G. Leverett (#110078)

ASCD myTeachSource®

Download resources from a professional learning platform with hundreds of research-based best practices and tools for your classroom at http://myteachsource.ascd.org/

For more information, send an e-mail to member@ascd.org; call 1-800-933-2723 or 703-578-9600; send a fax to 703-575-5400; or write to Information Services, ASCD, 1703 N. Beauregard St., Alexandria, VA 22311-1714 USA.

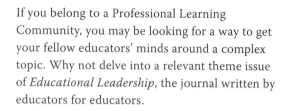

WHOLE CHILD
TENETS

1 **HEALTHY**
Each student enters school healthy and learns about and practices a healthy lifestyle.

2 **SAFE**
Each student learns in an environment that is physically and emotionally safe for students and adults.

3 **ENGAGED**
Each student is actively engaged in learning and is connected to the school and broader community.

4 **SUPPORTED**
Each student has access to personalized learning and is supported by qualified, caring adults.

5 **CHALLENGED**
Each student is challenged academically and prepared for success in college or further study and for employment and participation in a global environment.

The ASCD Whole Child approach is an effort to transition from a focus on narrowly defined academic achievement to one that promotes the long-term development and success of all children. Through this approach, ASCD supports educators, families, community members, and policymakers as they move from a vision about educating the whole child to sustainable, collaborative actions.

With the Whole Child in Mind relates to all five tenets. For more about the ASCD Whole Child approach, visit **www.ascd.org/ wholechild.**